FAITHFUL FINANCE
Money Essentials & Biblical Principles

To: Shawna

FAITHFUL FINANCE
Money Essentials & Biblical Principles

Emily G. Stroud

EMILY G. STROUD, MBA, CFA

Copyright © 2015 by Emily G. Stroud
All rights reserved. No part of this publication may be reproduced, distributed, or transmitted in any form or by any means, including photocopying, recording, or other electronic or mechanical methods, without the prior written permission of the publisher, except in the case of brief quotations embodied in critical reviews and certain other noncommercial uses permitted by copyright law. For permission requests, write to the publisher at the address below.

Fedd Books
P.O. Box 341973
Austin, TX 78734
www.thefeddagency.com

Published in association with The Fedd Agency, Inc., a literary agency.

Unless otherwise indicated, Scripture quotations are taken from the *Holy Bible, New International Version*®, NIV®. Copyright © 1973, 1978, 1984, 2011 by Biblica, Inc.™ Used by permission of Zondervan. All rights reserved worldwide. www.zondervan.com. The "NIV" and "New International Version" are trademarks registered in the United States Patent and Trademark Office by Biblica, Inc.

Scripture quotations marked [NLT] are taken from the *Holy Bible*, New Living Translation, copyright ©1996, 2004, 2007, 2013 by Tyndale House Foundation. Used by permission of Tyndale House Publishers, Inc., Carol Stream, Illinois 60188. All rights reserved.

Scripture quotations marked [KJV] are from T*he Authorized (King James) Version*. Rights in the Authorized Version in the United Kingdom are vested in the Crown. Reproduced by permission of the Crown's patentee, Cambridge University Press.

ISBN: 978-1-943217-13-7
eISBN: 978-1-943217-14-4
Jacket Design: Lauren Hall
Cover Photograph: Peter Robbins
Printed in the United States of America
First Edition 15 14 13 10 09 / 10 9 8 7 6 5 4 3 2 1

*To God and to all of those who try and be faithful to Him—
even with their money.*

TABLE OF CONTENTS

Introduction..9

CHAPTER 1..13
Let a Professional Worry About Your Money So You Don't Have To

CHAPTER 2..25
Cash Is King (or Queen)

CHAPTER 3..35
Pay Yourself First

CHAPTER 4..45
God is a Good Gift Giver

CHAPTER 5..55
Do Not Borrow from Peter to Pay Paul

CHAPTER 6..63
Nobody Got Rich Paying Too Much for a House

CHAPTER 7..75
A Penny Saved May Be More Than a Penny Earned

CHAPTER 8..89
Do Not Put All of Your Eggs in One Basket

CHAPTER 9..99
My Kids Want to Go to College. Now What?

CHAPTER 10...107
Is Your Life Insured?

CHAPTER 11...119
If You Ever Become Disabled, How Will You Pay Your Bills?

CHAPTER 12...129
Growing Older is Easier With Some Extra Help

CHAPTER 13...137
When Can I Transition from Making Money to Spending it?

CHAPTER 14...147
Proper Estate Planning is a Great Legacy

CHAPTER 15...157
God Will Provide—It May Just Look Different than What We Imagined

Conclusion 163

INTRODUCTION

Come to me, all you who are weary and burdened, and I will give you rest.

Matthew 11:28 NIV

God has laid it on my heart to help guide you on a path to financial freedom. As a financial advisor for over 17 years, I have observed that financial issues are one of the greatest stressors or burdens, for individuals and married couples. Sadly, it is one of the top three reasons that couples divorce. Issues with money cross all genders, races, and belief systems, proving that the fears associated with money do not discriminate. Those who don't have enough money to provide necessities for their family are often consumed with their personal finances. Surprisingly, those who do have plentiful resources are *also* concerned about their personal finances. You may be surprised to learn that my wealthy clients whom I counsel are often the most fretful people I meet. Those who do not have enough money and those who do have money are both worried about personal financial issues. It's epidemic.

Thank God there is *hope* in Christ. Jesus came so you could have access to *all* of God's blessings and treasures—all of them. My sincere desire is to share with you how to handle your finances so you can live without fear and anxiety.

Money is a tool to be used wisely and it can be a blessing to you. Those who are obedient to God's plan for their finances will be blessed, and will also be able to bless others. However, God's blessings look different for everyone. Please understand, I am not preaching a Prosperity Gospel. I am not promising that you will be rich beyond your wildest imagination if you believe in Christ, read this book, and follow my advice. However, I do want you to know that you can learn to manage money wisely and live a much more peaceful and fruitful life.

I also want you to know that the God of the Bible is good; the God of the Bible indeed blesses. The God of the Bible is the God who will see us through regardless of our stressful circumstances. God sometimes blesses our finances, and we raise our hands in thanks. But other times, we experience a lack of resources. Either way, God is always with us. He is watching and waiting for us to trust him, obey Him, and learn that in loving Him, we have life's deepest blessing.

Are you ready to go on this journey with me? Not only will we study God's Word, but we will also discuss practical ways to manage your finances. I'd like to end this quick introduction with a famous poem. Read it in light of your current financial situation:

God grant me
The serenity to accept
The things I cannot change,
Courage to change the things I can,
And wisdom to know the difference,
Living one day at a time,
Enjoying one moment at a time,
Accepting hardships as
The pathway to peace,
Taking as He did,
This sinful world as it is,
Not as I would have it,
Trusting that He will make
All things right if

Introduction

*I surrender to His Will,
That I may be reasonably
Happy in this life and
Supremely happy with
Him Forever in the next.
Amen.[1]*

1

Let a Professional Worry About Your Money So You Don't Have To

*Plans fail for lack of counsel, but with
many advisers they succeed.*

Proverbs 15:22 NIV

Frank and Diane have done an excellent job of managing their personal finances, even though they have experienced some very difficult trials in their lives. I had the privilege of meeting them for the first time during the spring of 2011.

Frank worked for a large oil and gas company for 34 years. In today's economy, people often move frequently from one position to another at various companies in order to climb the corporate ladder. Not Frank. He went to work for his employer in 1978 and retired on January 1, 2015. As a result, the majority of his net worth was tied up in his 401k plan, company pension, and corporate stock. Retirement for Frank was a bit scary because his work was a major part of his identity. Until that point in his life, his personal financial plan was quite simple: work hard and save as much money as possible. However, he soon realized that he needed a professional to coach him through the transition from working full time to retirement. He wanted to have a plan in place, and he certainly did not want to make any hasty decisions.

We held our first meeting at their modest, one-story ranch

style house. When I pulled into the driveway, they immediately welcomed me to their home. I soon learned that Frank and Diane had lived in the same brick suburban, ranch-style home for over 20 years. They made me feel comfortable immediately, offering a hug and no pretentious facade.

After a good bit of time, I asked them the following question: "What are your hopes, dreams, and desires for your retirement years?" Frank was rather young to be a retiree. I envisioned them volunteering at church, travelling, and spending time with their adult children and grandchildren at their lake house. But Frank and Diane's demeanor changed when we started to talk about the future. It seemed to me like they were living the American dream. However, the looks in their eyes left no doubt that something was indeed missing from this Norman-Rockwell-like picture.

Diane proceeded to tell me their story. "We have no children," she said. "So there will never be any grandchildren." At the time, I did not know that both of their children were deceased. Their youngest son had passed away at age 13 in 1999, and their older son died at age 20 in 2001. Both of their beloved sons had died suddenly and unexpectedly from previously undetected heart conditions. By this point in my career, I had counseled many people about how to handle their finances, hearing many personal stories about family dynamics, mismanagement of money, and fear about the future. I honestly thought I had heard it all. However, their story was something I had never heard before, or even imagined. To not only lose one child, but both, was difficult to grasp. How could a good God let this happen to them—twice? Initially, I had no words.

Yet Diane was not bitter. She lived at peace with her circumstances. She didn't pretend that the subject was not painful. However, she certainly was not depressed, angry, bitter, or withdrawn socially. I asked, "How have you survived the death of each of your sons? I honestly cannot imagine such grief."

She looked at me and said words I will never forget: "Emily, my faith is in Jesus Christ. This is not my home. My earthly life is temporary. I am at peace knowing that both of my boys loved Jesus. As a parent, that is the most important thing in the world. I

Let a Professional Worry About Your Money So You Don't Have To

know we will be together again so I have made a conscious choice to never become bitter. I want to make sure my boys recognize me when we meet again in heaven for eternity. If I become angry or bitter, they might not recognize me or know who I am at our reunion." As you can see, Diane demonstrated an amazing testimony of grace, poise and most importantly, genuine faith. God clearly uses her to minister to those experiencing great loss and tragedy.

Frank also uses their testimony to help bring young boys to Christ. He teaches Royal Ambassadors at their church and reminds each boy that he is not invincible. He explains that the best gift they can give to their parents is a relationship with Jesus Christ. Through Frank and Diane's lives, God has brought beauty from ashes.

Frank and Diane understand the importance of perspective when it comes to their legacy, but not everyone has such a solid foundation. In fact, many worry incessantly about their futures. That kind of stress robs them of joy today. Fretting about money causes people to lay awake at night worried about their future. The most common questions I hear regarding money are:

- How will I afford to send my kids to college?
- When will I have enough money saved to be able to retire?
- What will happen if I have an unforeseen illness or disability?
- Do I have enough life insurance to take care of my loved ones if I die before my children are raised?
- Why do I need a will?
- Who can I trust to give me personal financial planning advice?

Can you relate to any of these questions and concerns? Financial advisors don't just manage money. We manage relationships. We coach individuals and couples through all of the various stages of life so they can live their best possible life. Finances must be in order for people to feel at peace.

As part of the comprehensive financial planning process

outlined in this book, we will discuss all of the following topics:

- Monthly Budgets
- Personal Savings Goals
- Tithing
- Debt Management
- Purchasing a Home
- Investments
- Insurance Needs
- Retirement Planning
- Estate Planning

Each and every one of these topics will affect you and your personal finances at some point during your lifetime. Here is a brief overview of what these terms actually mean and how they relate to you personally:

Monthly Budgets

Do you know how much money you spend each month? If not, do not be embarrassed. Let's figure it out together. I suggest going to an all cash system for a couple of months to track your expenses. If you are very disciplined, you can use a shoebox and save every single receipt for a month. Do not leave anything off of your list. Put the shoebox next to the door of your home. Then empty your receipts from your purse or wallet every time you come home. If you spend $4.50 at your local coffee shop, then save the receipt. This is the only way to truly know how much money you are spending each month. After this, you will be able to determine how much discretionary income you have. Discretionary income is the amount of money you can afford to save each month after all of your expenses are paid. Be prepared to be surprised. Many people are shocked to find out how much money they spend on miscellaneous items like lattes, dining out, shopping, or entertainment. None of these expenses are bad. You just need to make sure you are spending *less* than your make. The goal is to have money left over each month to allocate towards your savings goals.

Personal Savings Goals

Goals are extremely important because they give you direction. If you do not have a plan, you will inevitably lose focus. As a result, you won't make wise decisions with your finances. There is a major difference between savings needs and savings wants. For example, you may need to save for your retirement and your children's college tuition. You also may want to save for a new car or a lake house. Both types of goals are good. However, savings needs should always take precedence over savings wants.

Tithing

The New Testament talks a lot about the importance and benefits of giving. We are to give joyfully as we are able. Why? Because all of our resources ultimately belong to God. We are just managers of the assets He has temporarily given to us. Sometimes that means giving more than 10 percent; sometimes that may mean giving less. People often argue about whether the Bible intends for you to give 10% of your Gross Income or 10% of your Net Income. Honestly, that is between you and God. Tithing is supposed to be a form of worship to God and service to the body of Christ.

Debt Management

This is a crucial part of financial planning. Not all debt is bad. However, you must be very prudent when using debt to improve your overall net worth. You may use credit cards for convenience purposes and reward programs to earn airline miles. However, you need to pay the balances on your credit cards in full each month. If not, you risk spiraling into stressful debt.

Purchasing a Home

A home may be one of the largest investments that an individual or a couple will make in a lifetime. It is possible to consider the practical housing needs of your family *and* make a very wise investment. As with all investments, ideally you want your asset to grow and increase in value, and not experience large swings in value or volatility. In the financial world, we call this: upside growth potential with downside protection. For many, a home will represent a large percentage of their assets and overall net worth. For more information, read Chapter 6.

Investments
This is a very broad topic, with more options for investing money today than ever before. Investing can be very overwhelming if you are not working with a professional Money Manager. However, do not be discouraged if you are just starting to save money. I will outline simple ways to begin investing—like purchasing well diversified mutual funds.

Insurance Needs
Protecting yourself and your family from a risk standpoint is the purpose of insurance. You can purchase insurance for life, health, disability, as well as personal property such as: a home, car, or boat. In most circumstances, insurance is not an investment; it is an expense. One exception to this rule is certain types of life insurance. However, for the most part, you want to provide insurance for yourself and your family for as little premium cost as possible.

Retirement Planning
Ideally, an individual or a couple will begin saving for retirement long before they actually plan to retire. The earlier you begin saving for retirement, the less you will have to save each month because you will take advantage of the beauty of compound interest. We will discuss retirement planning in much greater detail in Chapter 13.

Estate Planning
Estate planning consists of wills, trusts, and life insurance. You may need to work with a licensed estate planning attorney to ensure that your wishes and desires are carried out upon your death. There is never a good time to talk about death and after

life issues. Yes, it sounds morbid. However, I encourage my clients to embrace the fact that one of the best gifts they can give to their family is to have their financial affairs in order.

There are a lot of topics to cover to make sure your personal finances are properly managed, I sincerely want you to look forward to retirement, but I don't want you to spend your entire life pining for that one day when you no longer have to work. Worry like that is a waste of a valuable life. Let's start planning for *living* your best life possible now, and not for dying.

By now, I imagine you are probably wondering what proper financial planning looks like in real, every day life. You are probably also wondering if having a financial advisor really would be helpful for your own situation and personal finances. After all, everyone's situation is different.

Frank and Diane both continue to heal as they embrace a retirement that does not look like what they envisioned in their younger years. As I've mentioned, we have spent a lot of time discussing how to best use their time and resources during retirement. In order to illustrate how a financial advisor could help you, let me outline the various ways Frank and Diane organized their financial lives to get them ready for retirement:

Long Term Care Insurance
One of the first things they did was make sure that they purchased long-term care insurance. This covers any medical needs that may arise in the future, since they have no living children to help care for them if necessary.

Budget
Frank and Diane also made a very detailed budget for all of their monthly expenses during retirement. This is a very important step in planning for the future. Your budget usually changes quite a bit after you stop working. They practiced living on this new budget for a year before Frank actually retired to make sure it was realistic.

Will
Frank and Diane also met with an estate planning attorney to update their wills and trusts.

Annuity
An annuity is a guaranteed income stream, usually for a lifetime. In this particular situation, Frank and Diane annuitized a portion of their assets, in order to create a guaranteed income stream that they will never out live.

Emergency Fund
They also have a cash reserve to cover any unexpected financial issues that may arise.

Mortgage
When Frank first retired, he used a lump sum of cash from his 401k plan to pay off their mortgage so they would be debt free. They planned to stay in their existing home as long as possible.

Investments
With help from a professional money manager, Frank put an investment plan in place that is extremely well diversified. He wanted their assets to keep up with inflation and have upside potential. However, he also needed to provide their investment portfolio with downside protection since they are now retired.

I encouraged Frank and Diane to enjoy the fruits of their hard work. They are at peace knowing that they are financially secure. Remember, I encourage people to plan for living, not dying. I often say, "Go see the world. Travel. Check off some bucket list items." I am happy to report that they did go on a two-week Alaskan land excursion and cruise this past summer to celebrate Frank's retirement from the company. They marveled at God's creation and began to truly enjoy their retirement years.

I hope this story encourages you to seek wise counsel from a trusted financial advisor. Pray about the person whom you will hire to help navigate your path to financial freedom. Ask people you trust for personal recommendations. Be purposeful about handling your finances. You do not want to be a person tossed by the wind like the waves in the ocean. "If any of you lacks wisdom, you should ask God, who gives generously to all without finding fault, and it will be given to you. But when you ask, you must believe and not doubt, because the one who doubts is like a wave of the sea, blown and tossed by the wind." (James 1:5-6 NIV)

One question I am often asked is this: What qualities should I look for when interviewing prospective financial advisors? It may seem very difficult to choose an advisor among the thousands of people working in this industry. Advisors understand this dilemma so they have tried to differentiate themselves with various professional designations. These designations are displayed as three letters after the advisor's name, indicating which advisors have gone that extra step to make themselves qualified professionals.

Most designations are earned through required coursework and examinations that test an advisor's knowledge in various specialized areas. Some designations are specifically designed for financial advisors who work with retirees, while other designations show specialization in insurance or business. No two designations are exactly the same. Some designations are definitely more renowned than others.

If you don't know what a designation stands for and what it actually means, it can be difficult to know if the person really is qualified to manage your money and give you sound financial planning advice. FINRA is the National Regulatory Authority for the Financial Industry. They have an online resource that defines the various professional designations that advisors may hold. You can find this information at: www.FINRA.org.

For example, the letters after my name are MBA and CFA. MBA stands for Master of Business Administration. I earned this degree from Texas Christian University (TCU) in 1998. Only individuals who have finished the course work required for a graduate degree through an accredited university, focused on Business, can use the three letters: MBA after their name.

The second set of initials after my name is: CFA. CFA stands for Chartered Financial Analyst. I personally earned my CFA Charter in 2002. The CFA® designation is only awarded after the completion of three independent exams, usually occurring annually. The process is rigorous and demanding. In fact, during the period of 1963 through 2013, just over one million people have taken the first level of the CFA® exam and only 42% have passed. Additionally, over the same period, the pass rates for levels two and three are 46% and 59%, respectively. The rigor of the exams insures that the only candidates who pass are the candidates that should pass. Thus, only 164,000 candidates have earned the CFA® charter since 1963. Finally, and what is even more amazing, the percentage of women who earned a CFA® globally is only 19%. Just like any other financial advisor who has worked hard to differentiate themselves, I hope that understanding the value of the CFA® designation will help investors, readers, and my clients to recognize the significance of the knowledge that I can bring to help them manage their personal finances.

Be sure to check the educational background and years of experience of the advisor you choose to interview to manage your money. They should be well credentialed, not merely a good sales person. Check to make sure the advisor's security licenses are in good standing and that they have no fines or complaints filed against them. Some people in the financial services industry have taken intensive sales training programs. They can sell ice to an Alaskan. However, they do not have the knowledge, education, and experience required to truly provide you with wise counsel. As we say in Texas, "They are all hat and no cattle."

I would also encourage you to ask the people in your inner circle for a referral. It is always best to interview a financial advisor who has already worked for people whom you know and trust. Only use a fee-based financial advisor. Fee-based financial advisors do well financially if you do well, because they are paid a percentage of the value of the dollars that they actually invest. In the financial world, we call these dollars: Assets Under Management. The advisor's compensation will generally increase if your assets increase in value. If your account loses value, the fee-based financial advisor also generally earns *less* money. This is designed to prevent conflicts of interest. The annual fee charged by an advisor is usually around 1.0% of the assets under management. Similarly, do not hire a commission-based financial advisor, commonly known as stockbrokers without researching thier background and credentials. They only make money when they buy or sell a position in your portfolio. It may or may not be in your best interest for them to be constantly trading positions in your accounts. We call this "churning and burning." It is not a good thing.

Make sure the financial advisor has relationships with accountants and estate planning attorneys. It is best for all three advisors to coordinate your financial plan. You really need to know both the legal and tax ramifications of your investments.

It's optimal if your financial advisor is licensed to sell investments as well as insurance products. Life insurance, disability insurance, and long-term care insurance are very important aspects of your comprehensive financial plan.

Most importantly, make sure that the advisor is a person you truly like and want to spend time with. If the relationship is successful, they will become a major part of your life, one of the first people you call when any of the following major life transitions occur:

- Buying or selling a house
- Starting a family
- Kids going to college
- A family member passing away
- Changing jobs
- Starting a business
- Finally approaching retirement

You are going to do life with this person, so it is best if you enjoy their company and respect their opinions and advice. So be proactive and seek wise counsel with your personal finances. And remember what Benjamin Franklin said, "By failing to prepare, you are preparing to fail."[2]

2

Cash is King (or Queen)

But remember the Lord your God, for it is he who gives you the ability to produce wealth, and so confirms his covenant, which he swore to your ancestors, as it is today.

Proverbs 15:22 NIV

I first learned the importance of having a cash reserve during college. Be assured, I have not forgotten that very important lesson.

After I graduated with a Bachelor's Degree from Texas A&M University, I enrolled in a full time MBA program at Texas Christian University (TCU) in Fort Worth. As a result, I am an Aggie and a Horned Frog. In Texas, we call this dual-citizenship.

My parents were very generous to provide for my living expenses and my tuition as an undergraduate student. Upon graduation, my parents proudly shook my hand, congratulated me on all of my hard work, and joyfully told me I was on my own financially. My father literally skipped down the street. He kept shouting, "I just got a raise. Hallelujah. Both of my children are out of college." He called it Independence Day.

Sigh.

Needless to say, I was not nearly as exited as he was.

After graduation, I immediately started waitressing to earn

money while I waited to find out if I had been accepted to graduate school. I really thought that I had things under control financially when they awarded me a scholarship to pay for my tuition for two years while I attended the Masters Program. However, I did not know at the time that my fees and books were not covered by my scholarship. Unfortunately, I was not prepared for those unexpected expenses. There are two lines at the TCU bookstore to pay for your books. The first line is for students with Frog Bucks that enable them to charge their books to their parents' account. Students are very happy-go-lucky in that line. But there is a second line for students who were paying for their own books. I stood in that second line—the place where the real world got very real for me.

In order to keep my scholarship at TCU, I had to work on campus ten hours per week. I had hardly any margin in my week after I went to class, worked on campus, met with my peers for group projects, studied for exams, and read the required reading material. I managed to squeak by the first few months of graduate school on the money I had made during the previous summer waiting tables. However, by Christmas time I was almost broke.

I eventually finished my final exams after the first brutal semester of graduate school. All of us newbies in the MBA program were completely exhausted, sleep deprived, and barely able to think straight when our final exams were over. Then our professors handed us what they called a "Christmas Bonus." Unfortunately, it was not the financial kind. Our professors informed us that we had a group project to complete in three days. It was a Harvard Business Review Case Study where we read, analyzed, and then presented our findings to the faculty. They divided us into teams of five. I was the only member of my team who was not married, or did not have a roommate. Everyone agreed that my apartment would be the best place to set up shop since we would be awake for the next 72 hours.

And so it began...

My electricity was on almost 24 hours per day for three days. All of the lights in my apartment blared on, multiple computers were plugged in to remain charged, and my team members turned on my air conditioner during the day when they got hot. Then they would get cold at night and turn on the heater. Back and forth—hot to cold for three days. Why not? They were not paying for the electricity in my apartment.

I got my monthly electricity bill a few days after I went home to my parents' house for the Christmas holidays. Unfortunately, I did not have enough money in my checking account to pay the bill. I was now officially flat broke. So, I immediately had to get a job working over the Christmas holidays to make enough money to keep the electricity in my apartment on. My dreams of relaxing and recuperating from the difficult first semester of graduate school quickly shattered. Before the second semester began, I knew I would have to get another job in order to survive financially. Eventually, I figured out how to make it all work, but it was not easy. Desperation became a great motivator.

I did get a second job working for American Express Financial Advisors as an intern. Ironically, that is where my financial career began. If I had not been completely broke, I never would have agreed to take on another job, in addition to my on-campus job, and my full time graduate school schedule.

God had a plan all along.

And now I help others de-stress their finances. The very first question I ask my clients when we sit down for our initial conversation is, "How much cash do you have on hand?" It really does not matter if they want to talk about retirement planning or whether or not they have enough life insurance if they have no liquidity. One of the greatest stressors in America regarding personal finances is living over-extended. This is one of the reasons that credit cards were invented. People who live paycheck to paycheck, never quite get ahead because they do not have a cash reserve account. A cash reserve account is money you need to have on hand to pay for unforeseen expenses. I can promise you this: you are not in control. Things will break; people will get sick; and disasters will happen. If your refrigerator suddenly breaks, or you receive a very large unexpected medical bill, life will be very stressful without any cash to fall back on to pay for these expenses.

Rest assured, it's not all bad news. You absolutely can plan for these types of events in advance. If you have at least three months' worth of living expenses in cash, then life will become much less stressful. There is a lot of truth in the old saying, "Everything in life is easier with a little cash." Let's talk about the best way to build up an adequate cash reserve, and what to do with your cash once you have it in the bank.

Step 1
Review your monthly budget to determine exactly how much you are spending each month. I have created a detailed monthly budget worksheet for your reference at the end of this chapter.

Step 2
After carefully reviewing your budget, identify which expenses you regularly incur that are unnecessary. For example, eating out in restaurants or going to the movies are not necessary for your daily survival. As I mentioned earlier, these are called discretionary expenses. Remember, these activities are not bad, you just don't need these activities in order to survive. Try to think of ways to entertain yourself without spending money. Go for a walk; visit public parks, enjoy local playgrounds if you have children or grandchildren; attend activities at your local church; read a library book; or call a friend. You can even check out movies at the library for free. Get creative.

Step 3
Once your discretionary expenses have been identified, try to forgo as many of these expenses as possible. Use the money you would have spent on discretionary expenses to start funding a cash reserve account.

Step 4
Take an inventory of your possessions. Do you own anything you no longer need, use, or want that could be valuable to someone else? You may be able to clean out some clutter in your home

and turn it into cash. Simplifying is a great way to get your home more organized and start funding your cash reserve account. It will be a double blessing to you and your family.
Here are a few easy ways to make a little extra cash:

- Clean out your home and have a garage sale. Invite friends and family members to participate.
- Sell good quality clothes to a resale shop.
- If you have children, do you have any baby gear, toys, or clothing that your children have outgrown? Many communities have large swap meets for children's items that are used, but still in very good condition.
- Of course, there are many more things you can do to declutter and raise some extra cash. Once again, be creative.

Step 5
I recommend opening a savings account at your local bank that is separate from your regular checking account so the funds don't comingle. Why? Because it is very tempting to spend extra cash that sits in your regular checking account.

Step 6
Continue to save your discretionary income until you have at least three months worth of living expenses in your new savings account. This new savings account is now earmarked for emergencies only. This is not a rainy day fund to use if you suddenly have a desire to take a vacation or buy a boat.

Step 7
After you have three months of cash in your savings account, don't stop saving. You have now become much more disciplined in managing your monthly budget. Most likely, you have not even missed the funds you have been saving each month.

Step 8
Consider contributing your regular monthly savings to a new

investment account. You will want to grow these funds to keep up with inflation so they appreciate in value. There are many options for investing your money when you first begin. We will discuss investment options in much more detail in Chapter 7.

Step 9
Relax and enjoy your new financial freedom in regards to unforeseen expenses.

If you are uncertain about whether or not your job is stable, then consider setting aside six months worth of living expenses. This is also a good benchmark for people who are self-employed, or executives who work on commission only. If your income fluctuates from month to month, you will be better prepared financially to handle any swings in your income if you have adequate cash on hand.

My prayer for you is that you will be encouraged and inspired to build up and maintain a cash reserve account. I do not ever want you, my friend, to be one flat tire or other unforeseen expense, away from being flat broke. I want you to be protected from financial hardships in the future by being proactive with your finances. Please take some time to complete the detailed budget worksheet at the end of this chapter.[3] You can also find a downloadable version on my website, www.EmilyGStroud.com. It is the first step that you can take today to becoming financially independent. Don't forget: Cash is king (or queen.)

Monthly Budget Worksheet
Monthly Cost

Housing

Mortgage or rent	$0
Second mortgage or rent	$0
Phone	$0
Electricity	$0
Gas	$0
Water and sewer	$0
Cable	$0
Waste removal	$0
Maintenance or repairs	$0
Supplies	$0
Other	$0
Subtotals	$0

Insurance

Home	$0
Health	$0
Life	$0
Other	$0
Subtotals	$0

Transportation

Vehicle 1 payment	$0
Vehicle 2 payment	$0
Bus/taxi fare	$0
Insurance	$0
Licensing	$0
Fuel	$0
Maintenance	$0
Other	$0
Subtotals	$0

Food

Groceries	$0
Dining out	$0
Other	$0
Subtotals	$0

Children

Medical	$0
Clothing	$0
School tuition	$0
School supplies	$0
Organization dues or fees	$0
Lunch money	$0
Child care	$0
Toys/games	$0
Other	$0
Subtotals	$0

Entertainment

Video/DVD	$0
CDs	$0
Movies	$0
Concerts	$0
Sporting events	$0
Live theater	$0
Other	$0
Subtotals	$0

Pets

Food	$0
Medical	$0
Grooming	$0
Toys	$0
Other	$0
Subtotals	$0

Loans

Personal	$0
Student	$0
Credit card	$0
Credit card	$0
Credit card	$0
Other	$0
Subtotals	$0

Taxes

Federal	$0
State	$0
Local	$0
Other	$0
Subtotals	$0

Savings & Investments

Retirement account	$0
Investment account	$0
College	$0
Other	$0
Subtotals	$0

Monthly Income

Income 1	$0
Income 2	$0
Extra income (trust, royalties, etc.)	$0
Total monthly income	**$0**

Gifts & Donations

Tithe to Church	$0
Tithe to Charity	$0
Special Gifts	$0
Subtotals	$0

Monthly Income

Total Monthly Income	$0
Total Monthly Expenses from all Categories	$0
Difference = Discretionary Income	**$0**

Legal

Attorney	$0
Alimony	$0

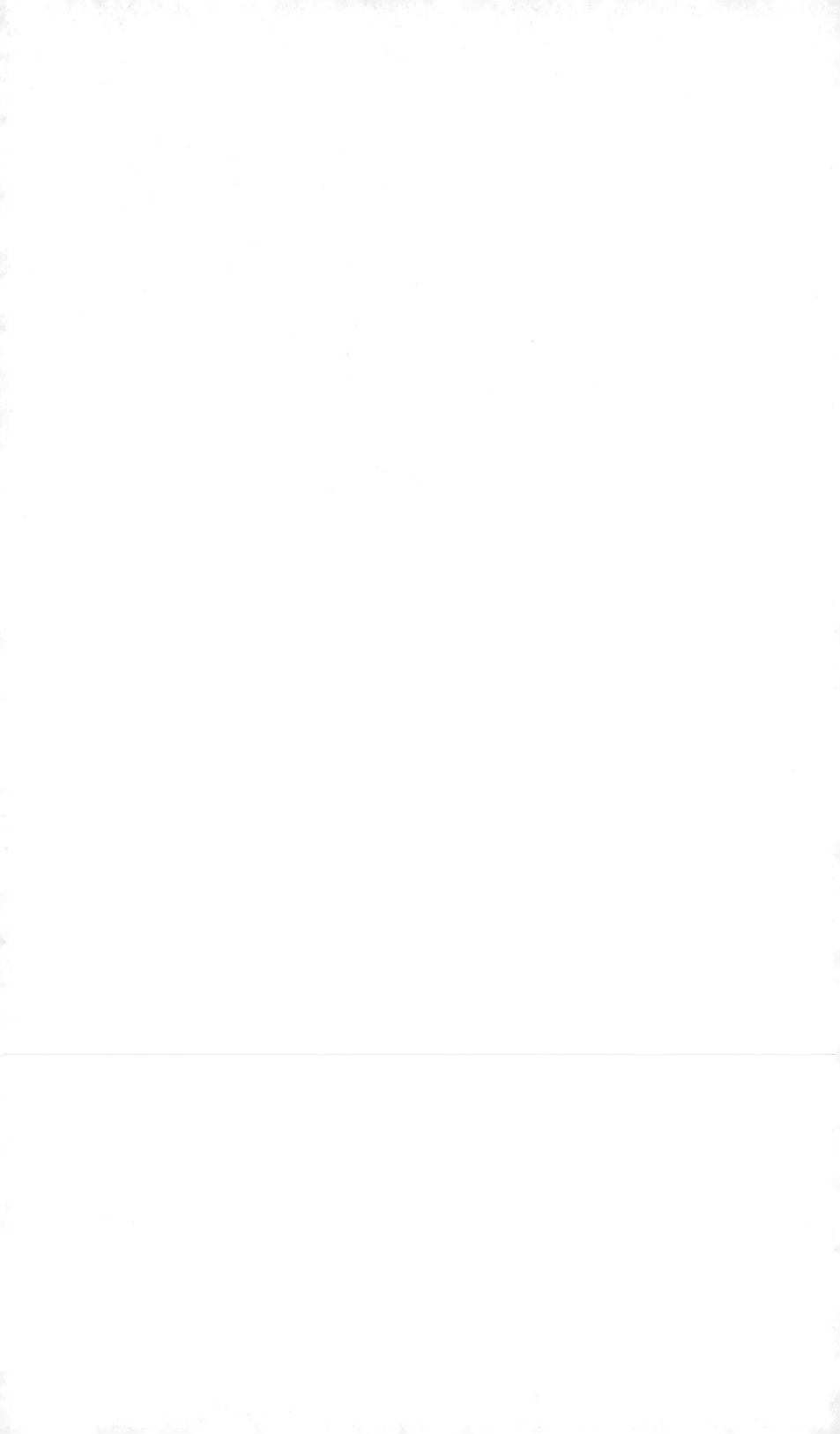

3

Pay Yourself First

The wise have wealth and luxury, but fools spend whatever they get.

Proverbs 21:20 NLT

Frank P. Carvey (originally Frane Carevic) was born on September 29, 1888 in the village of Selca on the island of Brae. The island of Brae is just a short distance in the Adriatic Sea from Split, Yugoslavia. However, it wasn't Yugoslavia then, it was Austria-Hungary. Frank was the oldest of ten children.

Frank's family was very poor and there were many mouths to feed. In 1902, the family vineyard and olive trees didn't produce much to live on, so it was decided that Frank should come to America. He was only fourteen years old when he made the risky voyage to America to find work to help support his family.

When Frank first arrived, he went to San Francisco to work for an uncle there who had a restaurant. Frank's uncle provided him with a place to live and he was able to eat at the restaurant where he worked. Frank saved as much money as he possibly could. This was his choice. He knew beyond a shadow of a doubt that he wanted to grow up and get married, have a family, and enjoy a better life in the United States of America. However, he never forgot his family in Yugoslavia. From the day he came to America, Frank assumed responsibility for his family. A part of every paycheck that he received, still a child himself, he sent back to his family in Yugoslavia.

Before he was twenty years old, he left his uncle in San Francisco to go out on his own. He continued a lifetime of association with the food business: first as a waiter, then a railroad dining car steward, then owning his own restaurant, to finally managing Lakewood Country Club in Dallas for twenty-six years, until his retirement from there in 1947.

After he found his way to Texas in 1910, he also found Ella Johnson, of Swedish parentage, and they married. He was 24 years old when his first child, Dorothy, was born in 1913. Frank and his wife Ella then had two more children: Helen, and Frank, Jr. This story is part of my heritage. Dorothy is my maternal grandmother. Had Frank not come to America as an immigrant in 1902, I would not exist. None of my maternal family would exist. He passed down a legacy to his children, grand children, and great-grandchildren that hard work was something to be proud of. He taught his family to save money, make wise choices financially, and to always give back to those in need. His legacy has lived on well past his death at the age of 94 in November of 1982. I was just eight years old at the time of his death, but I still remember the lessons he taught my family.

The story has been told to my family that when Frank's father died and his mother was alone with six children to support, she was forced to borrow money from a "money lender". This man asked her what she had to guarantee repayment of that loan. Her reply was, "I have money that comes from America every month." The man asked how she could be sure of that and she said, "You will see, you will see." And the money always came. And it continued to come, regularly. Even after his mother died, it came to his brothers and sisters that were left in Yugoslavia. During the hard, hard years between World War I and World War II, Frank's financial support meant life itself to his family on Brae. During World War II, when all of Europe was in such desperate circumstances, Frank sent care packages with flour, sugar, and other staples to the family. The food he sent literally kept them alive.

If my great-grandfather, Frank Carvey, could save money and help support his family as a fourteen-year-old immigrant, then you and I surely can save money as well!

I often get asked how to begin a savings plan. The hardest part is starting. Just like my great-grandfather taught my family, you have to make a choice to save regularly. You need to automate your savings plan so that money comes out of your bank accounts, or paycheck, systematically every month. If you wait to save money until the end of the month, I promise you will never have anything left over to save. As long as you consider saving money each month to be optional, you will have a difficult time being successful. Saving has to be a serious commitment and not negotiable. Consider making a monthly tithe to God who owns all of your resources, and then immediately pay yourself *before* you pay any other bills, or make any other purchases. You are your own biggest advocate for becoming financially independent.

People often procrastinate when starting a new savings plan. It falls into the same category as starting a new diet. You fear you are going to be restricted and miss out on the fun stuff. *Diet* and *save* are both considered to be ugly four letter words. "Let's eat that last ice cream sundae today, and then I will start my new diet plan tomorrow." But then tomorrow comes and you get asked to go out to dinner for Mexican food. "Oh well, one more day won't hurt to put off starting the new diet plan. Right?" And so on and so on…however, what you need is a lifestyle change, not a temporary diet.

The same goes for starting a savings plan.

Friend, accept your new assignment and start moving forward. Don't think of saving money as a punishment. Think of saving money as a means to *freedom*. It is a disciplined choice you can make today to benefit yourself and your family tomorrow. If you take control of your finances today, then you won't be a victim to them tomorrow. Nobody is making you save money *or* spend irresponsibly. By saving regularly, you are choosing a better life for yourself.

This new lifestyle may require supernatural strength to take a positive step forward. There are several ways to gather the strength you will need. Spend time in God's Word. Pray for wisdom, energy, and focus. Meet with someone you trust who can provide wise counsel and a rational sounding board.

It may seem over-simplified but there are three main ways to save:

Work more.
Want less.
Save more.

Work More

Working more does not just mean adding an extra shift to your already long workweek. However, some people who are heavily in debt may choose this strategy for a season until they get out of debt and get back on their feet. I promise you that you can do hard things if you know the extra work is only for a season and not forever. The long-term benefits will eventually outweigh your short-term fatigue.

What would happen if you started to think differently about the other four little word: *work*? Have you considered how to increase your income by doing something besides your regular day job, maybe something you're passionate about? Think outside of the employment box. Working more is also about being intentional with your time, talent, and resources. Think about your unique gift set and what gives you great joy. How could you leverage your specific gifts and talents to improve your financial situation?

Are you an excellent cook, or a great party planner? Are you an athlete that could earn extra money as a coach or referee? Are you good at needlepoint or monogramming? Can you use your skills to make specialty gifts and sell them for profit? The key is to determine which skills you have that are valuable to others. Then you have to research the appropriate amount to charge for your service or product. This will be a paradigm shift. You are going to trade your value and skill for someone else's money. When you use your gifts, you will find that work does not necessarily feel like *work*.

Have you completed your monthly budget worksheet at the end of Chapter 2? If not, this would be a very good time to complete that exercise. You really need to have a realistic budget for your expenses. We talked a lot about discretionary income and expenses in Chapter 2.

FORMULA: DISCRETIONARY INCOME = ALL INCOME SOURCES – ALL EXPENSES

By working more, you are increasing your discretionary income by increasing your total income stream.

Want Less

Now let's talk about ways to decrease your expenses. Are you spending money on stuff that has no long-term intrinsic value? If so, are you willing to make a choice today to simply want less stuff? This is a personal question. I want to encourage you to take some time and pray about this one.

In the USA, we have gotten into a habit of acquiring things first and then figuring out how to pay for them later. This is why the use of credit cards has become so popular. Credit card debt has become an epidemic problem for many people. The following statistics illustrate just how much people are using credit cards these days:

- Average credit card debt per U.S. adult, excluding zero-balance cards and store cards: $4,878.
- Average debt per credit card that usually carries a balance: $8,220.
- Average debt per credit card that doesn't usually carry a balance: $1,037.
- Average number of cards held by cardholders: 3.7 as of the end of 2009.
- Average APR on credit card with a balance on it: 13.01% in Q1, 2013.
- Total U.S. outstanding revolving debt: $856.5 billion as of May 2013.
- Total U.S. outstanding consumer debt: $2.8 trillion as of May 2013.[4]

We are buying things today that we cannot afford. Are you personally enslaved to credit cards? Are you worried about status symbols and appearing wealthy? Are you trying to keep up financially with other friends in your community, but struggling to do so? Are you trying to fill a deep-seated need in your life by overspending on stuff?

Friend, there will never ever be enough new stuff to satisfy you. Only God can satisfy your needs for love and self worth. God has placed emptiness in your soul that can only be filled by Him. Nothing money can buy will ever fill that emptiness. You may experience temporary happiness, but never lasting joy. Stuff will always rust, fade, break, go out of style, or become obsolete. Will you commit today to ask God for more of Him and less stuff? I want to encourage you to switch your focus from looking outward at the world and its trappings, to looking upward toward a God who loves you very much. Ultimately, you will find much more peace and lasting joy. Remember, "Keep your lives free from the love of money and be content with what you have, because God has said, "Never will I leave you; never will I forsake you." (Hebrews 13:5 NIV)

Save More

Changing your focus on a day-to-day basis may sound wonderful in theory but hard to implement. I have a very simple but practical cure for overspending. The first practical step you can take today is to make the choice to save more instead of spend more. The very stuff you are consuming to fill yourself up may be the exact thing that is causing you anxiety. If you will focus more on saving, and less on spending, you will experience financial freedom. Saving instead of spending will calm your spirit emotionally. You will rest easier at night knowing that you are helping yourself financially, rather than hurting yourself. This is what Jesus wants for all of us. He wants us to find peace and rest. Pray about your spending habits and ask God to reveal areas in your life where you are not being responsible with the money he has provided for you.

The second step is to categorize the items and services in

your life that are truly needs as opposed to wants. Wanting less leads to spending less money, which will ultimately allow you to save more. Don't delay the process. Start saving money as soon as you can. The younger you are when you start saving money systematically every month, the longer your money will be able to grow and take advantage of compound interest. I have found that most people can save more money each month just by being intentional about how they are spending their income.

The third step is to pay yourself first. Automate, automate, automate. Consider setting up an automatic draft from your checking account every single month on a specific day. Allocate a fixed amount to a savings or brokerage account. If you have adequate cash reserve already, start investing to grow your assets. Your age, resources, and stage of life will determine what your savings goals should be focused on.

In terms of savings, let's discuss what your goals and objectives should be for each decade of your adult life prior to retirement. Your age and your stage of life will largely affect what goals you should focus on.

Twenties

Your finances are most likely a lot simpler now than they will be in the future, when you may be juggling priorities like saving for a down payment on a house while also starting a family. Your 20s are an ideal time to establish good money habits that can help carry you through the next decades. I am often asked if new graduates should pay off credit card debt or student loans before they start saving for the future. My answer is: Yes. Always be proactive with paying off debt. However, split your discretionary income each month between debt service and savings, working on both goals simultaneously. Time is on your side. You have many years ahead of you to benefit from compound interest. In your 20s, your life is viewed as a marathon and not a sprint.

Your first savings goal should be a cash reserve equal to at least three months worth of living expenses for emergencies. As soon as you have a cash reserve account funded, start saving for retirement, even if you still have some debt to pay off. The earlier you start saving for retirement, the sooner you will achieve financial freedom. Then you will have options on how to spend your time. Trust me, the benefit of compound interest is something you do not want to miss out on in your 20s. You will want to monitor your accounts and goals at least once per year. Life will happen. You will have to make adjustments over time to your savings plan.

If you have a company sponsored retirement plan like a 401k, make sure you are contributing the maximum allowable contribution that you can afford. The maximum allowable personal contribution changes every year. In 2015, the maximum personal contribution was $18,000. Any matching funds your employer contributes to you personal retirement plan is free money to you. The employer's contribution is in addition to the $18,000 you are allowed to contribute. Remember, contributions to retirement plans are tax deductible.

Thirties

The financial decisions you made in your 20s, and the decisions you will make in your 30s, will have a large impact on your 40s, 50s, and beyond. During this decade, your financial goals are likely to get a bit more complicated. Many people are still paying off credit card debt and student loans, working on building emergency savings and kicking retirement savings into high gear—while also saving for a house down payment and perhaps thinking about starting a family. This is why it is so important to gain focus and be more prudent with your finances in your 30s. Make sure you keep a close eye on your budget so you can set up realistic savings goals for yourself and your family.

Big life events like getting married, having kids, or buying a house are important times to assess whether or not your insurance needs are being appropriately met. If you have children, securing long-term life insurance now will help them maintain financial security in the future if anything should happen to you. In addition, you'll probably have to plan for childcare costs, as well as starting to save for college. For the latter, consider opening a college savings plan and contributing what you can now to help defray tuition costs and other college fees down the road.

Forties

At this point in your life, you definitely want to be out of the credit-card-debt cycle and have any student loans paid off. As your income increases, do not forget to keep adding to your emergency fund if possible. Also, be sure to revisit your retirement projections, while also paying attention to other ways to grow your money.

If you have kids, you may be feeling the need to put your retirement savings on hold in favor of saving for college tuition. Do not let guilt lead you to make poor financial decisions. Remember, your kids can borrow money for college or work if necessary, but you cannot borrow money for retirement.

Although you may not have paid much attention to the asset allocation of your portfolio in your 30s, you've probably started accumulating some wealth by your 40s. These are typically your high-earning years, which makes it a good time to become more thoughtful about whether you're investing in the right way.

Fifties

A lot of events happen in your 50s: possible retirement, long-term care insurance for yourself, mortgage payments, and portfolio management. This stage of life is when you really need to be proactive with financial planning. Continue to revisit your savings and investment goals often. Now is the time to fully prepare for retirement, whether it's five years away or twenty years away.

At this point, try to save as aggressively as possible. Focus on reducing the risk in your investment portfolios, which can be accomplished by reducing stock holdings and increasing the percentage of bonds. Traditionally, stocks are considered more volatile than bonds. As you get closer to retirement, your emergency savings goal should now be one to two years of cash. The 50s can be the sandwich generation years. You may need to be supporting your kids while also taking care of aging parents. However, stay focused on your personal financial goals.

Consider the parameters of supporting grown children

financially before being confronted with a request. If you paid for every expense when your children were minors, proactively consider whether you will continue to contribute to your now young adult's expenses, like a down payment for a home or a graduate degree. This is not a decision to be made hastily because it may have long term effects on your personal retirement goals.

I have observed that many pre-retirees often underestimate their future financial needs during retirement, while also overestimating their current financial position. This is a classic reason why I want to encourage you to seek wise counsel and have a person you are accountable to, such as a financial advisor, or other person you trust.

I also suggest taking advantage of online calculators to determine how much you need to save to maintain your standard of living while in retirement. The math will not lie. The calculations will either confirm you are on the right track, or allow you to adjust your expectations for saving for retirement.

Friend, regardless of which stage of life you are currently in, I want to strongly encourage you to begin a savings plan, if you have not already done so. It is *never* too late to start saving. Then continue to monitor your goals and savings needs throughout each decade of your life. Systematic savings plans will make all the difference in relation to your stress level related to your finances. Just remember these three little words: Pay yourself first!

4

God is a Good Gift Giver

Every good and perfect gift is from above, coming down from the Father of the heavenly lights, who does not change like shifting shadows.

James 1:17 NIV

My friends Mike and Jessica are all about God's economy. They take their calling to provide provision for others extremely seriously. We recently met to discuss their thoughts and beliefs on giving generously. They were kind enough to share their thoughts openly and honestly with me.

Jessica is the daughter of a pastor who has always had a huge heart for others, but limited financial means. Jessica's parents modeled generosity by giving freely with their time and their resources. Jessica also had the opportunity to go into the mission field right out of high school. She was born with the spirit of generosity, but she had no idea how that would play out.

While working as a missionary in orphanages in Asia, she learned the gift of compassion. She spent time rocking malnourished toddlers, tied to chairs with string. No one touched them, so they failed to thrive. Jessica went from chair to chair untying these babies, feeding them, rocking them, and praying over them. The worst part? She had to tie the toddlers up again before she left.

From that point on in her life, she knew she could not pretend that suffering was not happening in the world, locally, nationally, or internationally. Jessica has always believed that giving is not just something that you do with a portion of your income and time. Instead, she believed that giving was her God-given purpose and the reason for living.

In 1998, she met her soon-to-be husband Mike. However, his background and spiritual gifts were far different from Jessica's. Mike was born into a family of entrepreneurs. His parents taught him how to run a business successfully, but they never taught him much about generosity. Mike's grandparents had survived the Great Depression. As a result, the legacy in Mike's family passed down for generations was to save as much as possible, in case another financial catastrophe ever happened again. Mike's family taught him to live in protection mode.

Mike and Jessica have been married for over fifteen years now. They have experienced huge financial success, as the world would see it. However, their business ventures have not always thrived, and they have not always lived on Easy Street.

After they first got married, Mike and Jessica bought a small business in a rural town in Texas and lived in an efficiency apartment. They struggled financially for many years. Mike spent a lot of time, energy, and sweat equity getting his business off the ground and making it profitable. A few years later, it finally generated enough income for Mike to net a modest profit. They were not wealthy by any means, but they were finally living a comfortable, middle-class lifestyle.

During this time, they made the decision to give above and beyond their tithe. They began to give sacrificially, regardless of the performance of Mike's business. Along the way, some crippling blows to the US economy devastated their financial reserves. Had they not given so generously, they may have had enough money to keep their business afloat. Mike grew angry with God. He questioned why God would allow this devastation when he and Jessica had been so faithful to give sacrificially. The irony of God's plan and provision came later after they had sold the failing company and invested in a new one.

As God would have it, by obediently tithing and giving as the Holy Spirit prompted, Mike and Jessica received the biggest financial blessing of their lifetime. A year after they sold the previously doomed business, their new business venture catapulted their income beyond their wildest dreams. They became millionaires in less than a year. Mike and Jessica then read *The Hole in our Gospel* by the President of World Vision, Richard Stearns. They had been very faithful to give a tithe and an offering throughout their marriage. But this book inspired and encouraged them to give even more sacrificially.

Stearns teaches in this book that God's answer to poverty is us. So Mike and Jessica began to give sacrificially, way above and beyond their 10% tithe. The Lord used the book to open their eyes to the fact that they had been given abundant resources, not to hoard for their family, but to give to those in need. As they accumulated more wealth, they became increasingly aware that there was no sports car, mansion, airplane or vacation home that came close to the eternal joy of giving to others in Christ's name.

It turned out that God was indeed blessing Mike and Jessica for their sacrificial giving. God actually *saved* Mike and Jessica from financial ruin *through* their generosity. Had they not been giving sacrificially, they would have had enough cash on hand to keep the original business that is now closed and worth nothing. The blessings of their faithful, sacrificial giving have been monumental both financially and spiritually.

Please understand that I am not encouraging you to give away so much money that you go bankrupt. I am not encouraging you to be irresponsible with your finances. However, I am encouraging you to give sacrificially. Mike and Jessica have inspired me by their faithfulness with their personal finances. They are investing in kingdom causes and not stuff.

The best news I have for you, my friend, is that our God is a good gift giver. Many people believe that they cannot afford to tithe to their church or give to those in need. They are fearful that they will not be able to meet their own needs if they give money to others. Trust me, God will provide for all of your needs. He may not provide for all of your wants, but He will always provide for your needs.

Part of achieving financial freedom is finally understanding that you will never prosper if you do not love others, as God has loved you. I love what Mother Teresa had to say about giving: "It is not about how much we give, but about how much love we put into giving."[5] You do not have to look very far to find people who are in need. Unfortunately, our natural, sinful nature is to look away, or run away, if we encounter people in need. Helping others can be messy, and we often don't want to be inconvenienced. However, Christ commanded us to show compassion and meet the needs as we see them, without expecting anything in return. "If anyone has material possessions and sees a brother or sister in need but has no pity on them, how can the love of God be in that person?" (1 John 3:17, NIV)

If we greet others with open hands, we will be opening our hands to accept new gifts from God as well. Author and motivational speaker, Zig Ziglar, developed a personal credo throughout his life and career that closely resembles Philippians 2:4: "You can have everything in life you want if you will just help enough other people get what they want."[6] To help yourself, you must first help others.

As I mentioned in Chapter 1, all of your resources ultimately belong to God. You are just a steward of the assets that He has entrusted you with. If you cannot be trusted to manage a small amount of money wisely, then why would God trust you with much? Jesus said, "Whoever can be trusted with very little can also be trusted with much, and whoever is dishonest with very little will also be dishonest with much." (Luke 16:10 NIV)

There is a lot written regarding the rules of tithing and the amount you are supposed to tithe each month. Historically, there have been many discussions about whether the Bible intends for you to give 10% of your gross income (Includes *all* income from all revenue sources) or 10% of your net income (revenue minus expenses and taxes).

I have also read articles discussing whether it is considered "stealing from God" to split your 10% tithe between the church and other charities. Another common debate is whether or not your acts of service count as a tithe. Honestly, I believe that how you spend both your money and your time is between you and

God. Tithing is supposed to be a form of worship to God and service to the body of Christ. If you focus too much on the rules of giving, you may become more focused on legalism rather than faith. At times, God may encourage you to give to a special situation, or an urgent need of someone in the Body of Christ. As a result, you will give more than 10 percent of your income. This is called an offering. It is money that you give over and above your 10% tithe to the church. There also may be extenuating circumstances during certain seasons of your life and that may mean giving less, or not at all. Instead, you will be the recipient of gifts and offerings from others as you handle an unforeseen crisis in your own life.

A friend of mine went through a medical crisis a few years ago that put a large financial strain on her family. Her husband had been laid off from his job for several months, and then she was unexpectedly diagnosed with breast cancer. She has told me that there was no way for them to tithe any money during that season of her family's life. However, up until that point in time, they had always been faithful to tithe and give to others. God did bring them everything they needed through the hands and feet of other believers. Many people gave sacrificially to help my friend and her family during her battle to overcome cancer. God blessed their generosity and faithfulness prior to her diagnosis with breast cancer. He did provide for their needs, even though the circumstances were extremely difficult emotionally, physically, and financially.

You may be surprised to hear this but God does not need your money. He is God. However, what He wants is a relationship with you and your heart. He wants you to be content with what you have and to give without compulsion. God wants you to be committed to giving generously even if it is not popular, easy, or returns anything to you. It has been proven that people who give generously to their church and to those in need, grow both spiritually and emotionally in the following ways:

- Faith grows, as you trust God with your resources.
- Depression and anxiety have been shown to decrease

as you learn to trust God more, and fear less about the future.
- You are blessed by being a part of something bigger than yourself. This results in a sense of community with others.
- Giving guards against the sin of selfishness.

As you learn to give generously, you will also become more content regardless of the circumstances around you. This contentment is only found in Christ. Contentment does not mean complacency. True contentment occurs when you are not using things or material goods to fill a void inside of your heart. According to Pastor Rick Warren:

> It feels good to give generously—it really does. A person who doesn't understand that has never given generously. The happiest people in the world are the most giving people. Guilt never motivates people to give. Giving that is motivated by guilt only lasts as long as the guilt does. So you never use guilt to motivate people to give. You use joy to motivate people to give. I absolutely do not accept the health and wealth theology, which teaches that God wants everybody to be rich. But the fact is, there are more promises in the Bible related to giving than any other subject. You cannot out-give God. If you're going to be Christ-like you've got to learn to give. Giving by revelation means I determine my gift by praying, 'Lord, what do you want to give through me?' This requires faith. When you give by revelation, you're committing an act of worship and saying, 'How much am I willing to trust God?'[7]

Let's talk about how to set up a plan for giving systematically so it is not a burden to tithe and give to those in need. I do believe it will become a true joy in your life, and your resources will multiply if you are faithful to give to God's church and His people regularly.

Step 1
Choose to tithe *not* because God will strike us with lightning if we don't (no, He won't), but because we love Him and have faith that He will take care of all of our needs. Tithing has nothing to do with money, but what the focus of our heart is.

Step 2
Be brave when you receive your next paycheck. Take 10% off of the top and ask God to bless your tithe to the benefit of His kingdom. Expect God to show up. Then wait and see if the rest of your bills don't get paid anyway. Prayerfully ask yourself, "Do I have more trust in my savings account to see me through life than God?" My prayer for you, my friend, is that you will have more faith and less fear in your life when you learn that God really does take care of us, no matter what. He knows every detail of the circumstances of your life. Rest in the fact that God is in control.

Step 3
If tithing does not fit into your current budget, do not be dismayed. Most people who tithe will tell you the same thing. "I don't know how it happens—it just does. Bottom line—tithing has nothing to do with my money, only my faith."

Have you ever heard of the difference between a king and a priest in God's economy? In my younger adult years, I somehow felt "lesser than" or "insignificant" compared to my family members who were dedicating their entire lives to full time ministry. Then one day I read David R. High's book, *Kings and Priests*. That one book changed my focus and helped me identify what God was calling me to do for His glory in my life. It was much different than what other members of my family had been called to do. All Christians cannot have pulpit ministries. If that were true, who would pay the bills? According to High, the wisdom God used to structure Israel can help us in the New Testament Church. Kings and priests are two very different callings.

The role of priests in Israel was to provide vision:

- Responsible for hearing from God
- Offered sacrifices on behalf of the people
- Received offerings and tithes from the people
- Took care of the house of God
- Took care of the widows and orphans
- Cared for strangers
- Encouraged people before battles

The Role of kings in Israel was to provide provision:

- Destroyed the enemies of God
- Took the spoils of war
- Paid tithes and offerings to the priests
- Governed the physical affairs of the nation[8]

If a king tried to do a priest's job, or vice versa, he suffered consequences from the Lord. The separation brought respect for both callings. My question for you is: *are you a king or a priest?* Take some time and pray about this question. Once you know for sure what your calling is, it may change the trajectory of your future.

The church needs to remember that kings who provide for the needs of the church are as valuable as the priests who hear from God and deliver sermons from the pulpit. God's kingdom on earth will go through a radical change if we will choose to honor and respect kings as much as we do priests. Teamwork between priests and kings will multiply God's blessings and the effectiveness of the church to meet more people with the Gospel of Jesus Christ.

I want to encourage you to research and pray about who God is leading you to support in your local community, in your church, or across the globe. God can use each and every one of us, no matter how large or how small our gifts are. If you currently have limited resources, do not be dismayed. You can still give of your time, and a portion of your income. My charge to you is to *just take the next step.* If you have never given anything to anyone, start with a small tithe. If you are already tithing, consider giving more sacrificially. Be an investor in kingdom causes. Your family will be blessed, and generations will change for the better through your tithes and offerings.

Let's be brave and be the change this world needs. And as we give sacrificially, let's remember the wise words of Malachi: "Bring the whole tithe into the storehouse, that there may be food in my house. Test me in this," says the Lord Almighty, "and see if I will not throw open the floodgates of heaven and pour out so much blessing that there will not be room enough to store it." (Malachi 3:10 NIV)

5

Do Not Borrow from Peter to Pay Paul

Give to everyone what you owe them: If you owe taxes, pay taxes; if revenue, then revenue; if respect, then respect; if honor, then honor.

Romans 13:7 NIV

I was a banker for many years. We worried about our customers that were overextended on their credit cards or lines of credit, especially at Christmas or Hanukkah time, the bastion of gift giving. Some customers did not adhere to a realistic budget when buying gifts for their friends and family members. It was pretty obvious by mid to late December that they were not going to be able to pay for all of the assorted gifts they purchased, often paid for with credit cards. It is not uncommon for people to become irrational and emotional spenders during the holiday season.

We had a saying at the bank during the holidays that I still remember to this day. We used to tell people, "Make sure you pay your bills so Repo Santa doesn't show up at your house this year." Repo Santa is Bad Santa at his worst. Nobody wants a visit from this jolly old man. Instead of giving gifts to you and your family, his job is to take back all of your new loot that you couldn't afford to pay for. I have a vivid picture in my mind of Santa Claus gathering up all of the presents under a Christmas tree and taking them *back up* the chimney because the gifts had not been paid for. What is the most common financial mistake that people make today? I bet you already know. It's not a new phenomenon. We are all inherently sinful and selfish by nature, so we want everything *now*. If we don't learn the concept of delayed gratification, or self-control, before we become adults, we can easily get into trouble financially.

It used to be that having a credit card was a luxury or a rarity, but now most households have several of them. We have the ability to get exactly what we want today, regardless of whether or not we can actually afford it. If we are not careful, we can become overextended on credit cards—quite a slippery financial slope. Just like any sin, a little is fun. We all like our stuff because it is exciting to get new things. Current studies regarding brain research show how shopping activates key areas of the brain, making us feel better and boosting our mood, at least temporarily. Gazing into a beautifully decorated holiday window, or finding a hard-to-find toy taps into the brain's reward center, triggering the release of brain chemicals that give you a "shopping high." This is where the term "retail therapy" comes from. If you are aware of the way your brain responds to shopping, it can help you make sense of the highs and lows of impulse shopping, avoid buyer's remorse, and lower your risk for overspending.[9] Shopping really can become addictive if you are not careful. Under a mountain of stuff and debt, you end up headed somewhere you never intended.

The Bible does not say that debt is a sin. However, debt essentially enslaves us to the one who provides the loan. Just like anything else that can be addictive if abused, a little is okay but a lot is overwhelming. At the same time, in some situations going into debt is a wise move financially. Debt can be used to purchase an item that will eventually lead you to financial freedom. Examples of good debts are mortgages to purchase a home, or loans to start a business that will provide income for your family. As long as money is being handled wisely and the debt payments are manageable, it is not sinful to take on debt.

As I mentioned earlier, in order to become financially independent, we have to save more money and spend less money. This is a paradigm shift for those who have made credit cards a normative practice. We are required to pay back what we borrow. It is easy to take this lightly, but if we borrow it, the debt is our responsibility to pay back.

There are various ways to obtain credit, or in other words, borrow money. You can obtain credit without any collateral, using credit cards or unsecured lines of credit, or you can get a secured loan that requires you to pledge some form of collateral. Let me explain the different types of lending options available today so you can be an informed consumer.

Credit cards

Credit cards are unsecured loans that allow the cardholder to borrow money on demand, usually at the point of sale, up to the maximum credit line he or she has available. The interest rate on credit cards averages 18-20% per year. Credit cards are quite expensive if not used responsibly for three reasons. First, the financial company providing the credit card charges the cardholder an annual fee to have the privilege of borrowing money on demand. Second, credit card companies charge interest on the amount borrowed if the cardholder does not pay off their outstanding balance in full each month. Third, financial companies make a lot of money every month because they charge late fees if the cardholder forgets to make the monthly payment on time. It does not matter if your payment is only one day late. They still charge a late fee. In light of this, always verify what day your bill is actually due and make sure you do not miss the deadline.

Unsecured Lines of Credit

These loans are very similar to credit cards but are issued by a bank. The interest rate is usually significantly cheaper than what credit card companies charge. If you do not use the line of credit to borrow any money, then you do not pay any interest to the line of credit. If a borrower has a very poor credit score, they are going to have a very difficult time obtaining this type of loan.

Secured Notes

These are loans that require collateral, which is an asset that the borrower offers the lender to secure the loan. If the borrower does not pay the required debt service payments, then the lender has the right to take the collateral. This process is called "repossessing an asset."

Car note

These loans are usually amortized over three to five years. The car the borrower purchased secures the loan.

Other Vehicles Loans

These are loans for boats, tractors, trailers, etc. They are structured very similarly to car notes.

Mortgage

A mortgage is a loan used to purchase a home that is secured by the entire value of the home. Interest rates for mortgages have historically been very low for over 15 years. If used responsibly, a mortgage loan is known as a "good debt." The loan allows the borrower to make an investment in real estate and purchase a home for their family. The interest on the mortgage is tax deductible up to a loan amount of $1,000,000.

Please be very careful of mortgage loans with unfavorable terms to the borrower. We call these predatory loans. One example is an Adjustable Rate Mortgage (ARM). "Amortization rate" sounds like a complex idea. However, it simply means the total number of months you have until the mortgage loan will be paid off in full. Normally, the amortization rate is 30 years (360 months) or 15 years (180 months). For a traditional mortgage, the interest rate is fixed for the life of the loan. However, an ARM will still have a 15 year or 30 year amortization schedule, but the interest rate will only be fixed for 5, 7, or 10 years. I see people get into trouble, especially with 5 and 7 year ARMs. If interest rates have risen significantly since you originally obtained the loan, the monthly mortgage payment can sky rocket overnight at the maturity date.

Another type of loan to be concerned about is a mortgage with a balloon payment. These also can get borrowers into trouble. A balloon payment mortgage does not fully amortize over the term of the note. There is a balance due at maturity of the loan called a balloon payment.[10] The reason they are attractive is the monthly payments are initially much lower. This allows people to afford more expensive homes. However, when the loan matures, the balloon payment, or simply the remaining balance on your mortgage loan is due in *full*. There is no problem if the borrower has enough cash to pay off the loan, or simply refinance the loan when it matures. However, what if you cannot afford to pay off the balance of the loan *or* get approved to refinance your loan? Then you are really in trouble.

Home Equity Loan
This is a loan that a borrower has access to if they have significant equity in their home. The terms are often very favorable. Just like a mortgage, the interest is tax deductible. People will take out home equity loans to make repairs on their home, pay for college, pay off debt, etc. The borrower is free to use the funds however they wish.

Home Equity Lines of Credit (HELOC)
Instead of a lump sum of cash, a HELOC offers homeowners a line of credit with a very low interest rate. The line of credit is collateralized by the equity in the home. This works like a credit card that you can use it as long as there is availability on the line of credit and pay it off as you wish. If you do not have any funds "drawn up" on the line of credit, then you do not owe the bank anything. Some people put these loans in place as a safety net for cash or liquidity emergencies. They do not plan to use the line of credit, but it is available if needed.

Home Improvement Loan
This loan is similar to a home equity loan, but the proceeds can *only* be used to make repairs and renovations to your home. You will be asked to show receipts for work completed on your home. Most likely, the bank will come out to the house periodically for inspections during construction. One major benefit of a home improvement loan

is that it can be refinanced and rolled into your traditional mortgage loan. In contrast, a home equity loan *cannot* be refinanced and rolled into a mortgage loan.

As you can see, there are a lot of different lending options available today. The debt we are always most concerned about consumers managing properly is credit cad debt. It is the most expensive way to obtain debt and very easy to abuse. Based on an analysis of Federal Reserve statistics, the average U.S. household credit card debt today stands at $15,863, counting only those households carrying debt. It is epidemic. If you use credit cards to borrow money to pay for things you cannot afford today, and you do not pay the balance off in full each month, it will take you many years to get out of debt. The credit card companies get richer while you struggle to get ahead financially. The following are five habits you can create that will help you conquer your debt spending.

Habit One
Make sure you have a realistic monthly budget. This helps you to remain focused on your spending habits. You know for sure what you can and cannot afford to buy each month.

Habit Two
Stop and think before you make a purchase. Often, it is a good idea to wait a few days after initially thinking about a purchase to determine if it is simply an impulse buy, or something that you, or your family, truly need.

Habit Three
Avoid the trap at many clothing and big-box retail stores to open up a credit card at the time of purchase in order to save 10%. Having lots of miscellaneous credit cards is not good for your credit score, and it encourages you to overspend.

Habit Four
Have a line item in your monthly budget for miscellaneous

purchases. I have many clients that keep cash for these types of scenarios. Once the cash is gone, you cannot make any more miscellaneous purchases until the following month.

Habit Five

Have a separate savings account for vacations. This is one of the major expenses that people put on credit cards because it is not part of their regular monthly budget. You may enjoy that week at Disneyworld, but spend the rest of the year paying off your credit card. This really steals the fun from a vacation.

In summary, my best best advice is to not make any decisions about large purchases or taking on debt without first praying about it. Do not make a decision and then ask God to bless it. Pray first and then take action as the Holy Spirit leads you.

6

Nobody Got Rich Paying Too Much For a House

Suppose one of you wants to build a tower. Won't you first sit down and estimate the cost to see if you have enough money to complete it?

Luke 14:28 NIV

My husband and I have actually made money in real estate. It has taken sweat equity and vision for how each home could look after being renovated. I'm grateful to say the work has paid off.

In 1998, my husband was in his early 20s. He decided early on that he wanted to invest in real estate. He was still a student on a very tight budget. He had to do his research and be very selective when he went house hunting for the first time. He definitely had to get a mortgage for his first real estate purchase. He ended up choosing a condominium in a great location but in very bad shape cosmetically. He and his parents used sweat equity to paint, replace carpet, lay hardwood floors, and change out doors and hardware in order to give the home a facelift on a very small budget. He did all of this before I even met him.

After we married, I moved into the condominium with my new husband. We quickly realized that a one-bedroom, loft style condominium was not very conducive to privacy. If one person worked or studied while the other person watched TV or slept, we had no sound barrier. So we sat down and analyzed our options. We met with a realtor that we trusted to find out how much we could realistically sell the condominium for. Then we researched the market to find out if we could afford a larger home, with at least two separate bedrooms.

We were excited to learn that my husband's sweat equity had paid off. He had made a very wise investment when he purchased his condominium in a very desirable location. However, if we really wanted to move into a larger home, we were going to have to buy a "fixer-upper" once again and use our sweat equity and profit from the sale of the condominium to do renovations and repairs. So, that is exactly what we did, and we were fortunate that it all worked out. God was very gracious to us.

But then life happened and we found out that we were going to move to a different city for career reasons. We would have to sell our new little bungalow before we owned it for two years, which would mean any profits we made would be subject to capital gains taxes. Not good news. We spent months updating our home, and we knew that we could potentially make a nice profit one day.

I did my research and sought wise counsel from an accountant. It turned out that there is an exception in the capital gains tax law if you have to move more than a certain number of miles for a job relocation. So, we were fortunate to be able to sell the bungalow for a very nice profit without paying any capital gains taxes.

And then we took the profit that we made from the sale of the bungalow and bought a larger, slightly more expensive house in a very desirable location when we moved again to a new city. This time we did not buy a fixer-upper. However, we bought a home that was vacant because the former owner was in the military and had been transferred overseas. A relocation company owned the house and they just wanted to sell it. For them, it was a non-emotional deal—the best type of seller. Most individuals who own a home are emotionally attached to it because their family has made special memories in the home. Homeowners often believe their house is worth more than it is actually worth, so emotional sellers can make the negotiation process much more difficult.

Since we knew the house we wanted to purchase was owned by a corporate entity, we made a very low offer, which was accepted. This particular home was one of the smallest houses in the neighborhood. We made sure the home was in an excellent school district for resale purposes even though we did not have children at the time. To make matters more interesting, there was a city zoning issue going on at the time we bought the house, related to some apartment complexes near this particular neighborhood. The home values were depressed a bit because people were nervous about the future property values. After a few years, the city and any potential buyers realized that the zoning issues were not a problem after all, and our entire neighborhood quickly escalated in value.

Once again, we made a wise investment in real estate and you can do the same. You just have to be an educated, non-emotional buyer. We stayed in this home for over five years. In the meantime, we became parents for the first time in 2006 to a sweet baby girl.

One beautiful afternoon in 2007, I decided that it was a great day to take the baby for a stroll around the neighborhood. Lots of our neighbors were outside when the weather was nice, and it was fun to stop and chat with people along the way. One of our neighbors had been unexpectedly widowed during the previous year. While I walked around the neighborhood, I decided to check in on him to make sure he was doing all right. He told me that he was actually doing great. As a matter of fact, he was engaged to be married again.

He had been married for over 50 years, and his wife had only been gone for about nine months. Quite a shock. *What are the odds of that?* I thought to myself. So, I did what every good "real estate agent" would do in that situation, and I calmly asked him if he planned to move or stay in his house after he was remarried—very key information. He lived in a corner house on the largest lot in our neighborhood with tons of potential. We had driven past his house multiple times every day for years. We had always thought with some modifications, his home could be a great fit for our family. Never in our wildest imagination did we think he would be moving out of his home, any time soon. Much to my surprise, he had already decided to sell his house once he figured out where he and his new wife would live after they were married.

So I went home and talked to my husband immediately. We knew all along that the house would need to be remodeled if we were to purchase it for our family. I told our neighbor not to do a thing to the house before he moved out, which he was thrilled about. This was a big blessing to him because he never had to go through the stress of putting his house on the market. We were able to purchase a home once again at a discounted price because it needed some work, and we did not use any real estate agents. He needed several months to get organized in order to actually move out. So he stayed in the house for about four more months. That allowed us the time that we needed to finalize our renovation plans with our architect and contractors.

Meanwhile, we sold our existing home for a very nice profit by word of mouth, without paying any real estate commissions. A wonderful family purchased it, and they were not in a hurry to move in. They graciously allowed us to rent our house back from them, and stay in our existing home until we finished the construction on the new house. Thankfully, we only had to move once, and God worked out all of the details. This was the first time we ever thought we were buying our "forever home." We often joked that we would be buried in the backyard because we were never going to leave.

That was the plan...or so we thought.

My husband and I are adamant that we be good stewards of the resources that God has given us. Our home falls into this category. We have always wanted to make sure if we moved, that is was God's best plan for us. Moving does not scare us. However, doing something that is clearly out of God's will really frightens us.

In 2010, we became parents again for the second time. This time we had a bouncing, baby boy. After a couple of years, we realized that he wanted to be outside running and exploring freely. By 2013, the "forever home" we were living in, was no longer conducive to our growing family's needs. We decided to do a little exploring. We found a house for sale on a good size piece of property with a fishing pond, only ten minutes from the heart of the city and all of its conveniences—something extremely rare, especially for the price. The house needed a major overhaul, but we love interior design so that actually was a bonus to us. By this stage of our lives, we had a lot of practice. We could modify the house for our taste and our family's needs. We asked God to confirm that this was in fact the right plan for us, before me made any decisions.

My husband had been saving money and planning for over a year to take his mother on a trip for her 60th birthday and his 40th birthday. They had their trip planned long before we decided to consider moving. I decided to put some feelers out to see if anyone might be interested in our existing home. I put some pictures of our home on Facebook and gave some details about the house. I told my "Friends" on Facebook to call me if they were interested in seeing the home in person.

My husband left to go out of town on a Saturday morning, and I showed the house twice that same afternoon. We had a contract on the house the following day and it was in escrow by Monday morning. God clearly confirmed that moving was in fact the right next step for us. So, as soon as he got back in town, we started making plans for the new home in the country.

The funny thing is, I cannot imagine living in a neighborhood now. I love the wide-open spaces and the beautiful scenery of living on land. We are very blessed to have neighbors with children on either side of our property. I ring a large, black dinner bell when it is time for the kids to come inside. The air is fresh, and my kids are learning how to climb trees and go fishing. We even have our own garden now, and the children are learning how to grow and harvest corn and other crops. We truly love to have family and friends over to our home, in order to relax and bless them.

I also now have a home office where I can work and still keep an eye on our children. Interestingly, I have found that clients who come to my new home office often stay a little longer, and seem more at peace after our meetings than when they first arrived at our home. My business has actually prospered more as a result. Who would have ever thought? Only God.

I recently talked with a friend who did not think that buying a house was an investment opportunity. She believes buying a home is more of a quality of life issue. In her opinion, you should simply purchase a home that is in a location, price range, and aesthetic that best fits your family's lifestyle. I respectfully listened to her theory and did not comment, but I could not disagree more. A house is a tangible real estate asset and definitely can be a good or bad investment. This really is not even a debate from a personal financial planning perspective. Buying a home may be one of the largest investments an individual, or a couple, will make in their lifetime.

Yes, you need to take into consideration your specific housing needs, such as the number of bedrooms your family may need, or finding a home in a good school district if you have children. You will definitely want to consider other lifestyle factors like:

- How long will your commute to work be if you live in a certain location?
- Do you prefer a home outside of town, in the suburbs, or do you want to live in the heart of the city?
- Do you want a two-story home, or do you need a one-story home because someone in your family has difficulty with climbing stairs?
- Is a large yard a priority or not?

My professional opinion is that you can consider the practical housing needs of your family *and* make a very wise investment with upside growth potential. For many people, the house they purchase will represent a large percentage of their assets and overall net worth. A house or condominium is tangible real estate and is a significant asset. Everything you own represents a portion of your overall net worth. Here's a simple formula:

Net Worth = Total Assets – Total Liabilities

You may not be aware of the fact that you can sell your primary residence after two years and pay no capital gains taxes on your profit up to $250,000. If you are married, you are exempt from capital gains taxes on profits up to $500,000. Please note that this tax law does not apply to second homes or investment properties. If you have a mortgage on your home, the interest and property taxes that you pay while you own the home are both tax deductible. Your home can be one of your largest assets and also one of your most tax efficient investments. However, it is very important to figure out a realistic budget before shopping for a home. This is not just a suggestion; it is sound, Biblical advice.

Wouldn't it be fantastic if everyone could afford to pay cash outright for a new home? If you can do this, please do. However, this is not realistic for a large portion of the population. Many people cannot afford to pay for their homes outright with cash. If you cannot pay cash for a new house, you will want to get pre-qualified for a mortgage before you start house hunting. Remember, you will also need enough liquidity, or cash on hand, to make a down payment. Find out how much you will need for a down payment before you start shopping for a house. If you cannot make a down payment, then you are not ready to start looking for a new house to purchase. You will need more time to save money for your down payment.

I am often asked, "Is it still a good idea to purchase a home, rather than rent a home, even if you need a mortgage loan?"

My answer is, "Yes." If you make a wise choice when you purchase your home, and it is in a price range that you can easily afford, then you will build equity in a real estate asset. Conventional mortgage loans are designed to be paid once per month for 30 years. I want to tell you about a simple strategy for paying off your mortgage early. Instead of paying your mortgage payment once per month for 360 months, I suggest that you split your monthly mortgage payment in half, and pay every two weeks instead.

Example
Annette purchases a home and has a mortgage balance of

$300,000. Her interest rate is fixed for 30 years at 4.5%. If she pays her regular monthly mortgage, she will make 360 monthly payments of $1,520.06 = $18,240.72 (principal and interest) per year.

However, Annette can pay her loan off almost 5 years earlier if she simply makes bi-weekly mortgage payments every two weeks, regardless of the day of the month on the calendar. There are 52 weeks in a year. Using this strategy, she will make 26 bi-weekly payments of $760.03 = $19,760.78. Using this strategy, an extra $1,520.06 will be paid each year to reduce the principal of her loan balance. As a result, her mortgage loan will be paid off 53.1 months faster and she will save $42,049.51 in interest expense. This strategy will allow her to pay her home off early and position herself for retirement with no house payment.

I do not consider a mortgage loan a bad debt. Please understand that I am not advising you to spend beyond your means. I am, however, advising you to make all of your money work as hard as possible so that you can achieve financial freedom. If you are responsible with your mortgage loan payments, you will eventually own your home outright. If you continue to rent indefinitely in order to avoid a mortgage loan, then you will never own a home.

As we discussed previously in Chapter 5, there is a big difference between what I consider bad debt and good debt. Bad debt encompasses credit card debt and other unsecured loans, which are loans that are obtained without the use of property as collateral for the loan. Bad debt also includes loans for cars, boats, or other types of vehicles that automatically depreciate in value the day you drive them off of the parking lot. Good debt is debt that is used wisely to purchase appreciating assets. If you make a wise purchase when you buy your home from an investment standpoint, your house will appreciate in value. Please remember that if you will have a mortgage on the home you wish to purchase, you must first make sure that you can comfortably afford the monthly payments. Otherwise, you should not be purchasing the home, even if it may appreciate in value one day.

Debt-to-Income (DTI) Ratio is a lending term that describes a person's monthly debt load in comparison to their monthly gross income. Mortgage loan officers use the debt-to-income ratio to determine whether an applicant can maintain payments on a given property. It helps both banks and prospective buyers to answer the question, "How Much House Can I Afford?"

The Debt-to-Income Ratio has nothing to do with the *willingness* of a person, or couple, to make their monthly mortgage payments. It simply measures a mortgage payment's economic burden on a household. Most mortgage guidelines enforce a maximum debt-to-income limit. Mortgage lenders calculate income a bit differently than most people. They consider more than just your take-home pay. They give a potential borrower credit for bonus income, certain itemized tax deductions, and also apply specific guidelines for part-time work. The simplest income calculations are used for W-2 employees, who receive no bonus, and make no itemized deductions.

Most mortgage lenders require homeowners to have a Debt-to-Income Ratio of 40% or less. Shockingly, loan approvals are possible with DTIs of 45% or higher. I do not recommend that your monthly housing budget get even close to 40% of your monthly income. I think this is a very slippery slope.

My professional recommendation is that your entire monthly housing costs should not be more than 25% of your overall monthly budget. I believe that this is a much safer option financially. You want to make sure that you always have adequate cash flow to cover all of your expenses. When figuring out how much house you can afford to buy, be sure to count all of your housing expenses, and not just the mortgage. You will have to pay property taxes every single year. This expense must be included in your overall housing budget. Property taxes can be a significant annual expense, depending upon the tax laws for the state in which you live. I also advise my clients to find out what the average cost of utilities will be for the home each month, and whether or not the home is located in a neighborhood or building that requires you to pay homeowner's dues and/or maintenance fees.

Once you have established a realistic housing budget, then you can start the fun part, which is house hunting. Do not look at homes that are over your budget. Be careful if you are working with a realtor who is not listening well to your specific requests. Many realtors are very persuasive and often try to push their clients up into a higher price point. The more money you spend on a home, the higher the realtor's commission will be, so it's not rocket science to figure out that they can have a conflict of interest. Definitely not all realtors, but some realtors, will show a prospective buyer a beautiful, sparkly, shiny house in a price range that they simply cannot easily afford. This is dangerous from a financial standpoint. Before you know it, you will be trying to rationalize in your mind ways to afford more house.

I am speaking from experience when I tell you that you can still enjoy living in your home, while making a wise investment. It does take discipline though. As I've shared, my husband and I have purchased several homes in very desirable locations that needed some work to bring the house back to life. We were able to "buy low and sell high" after we renovated the homes. If you purchase a home that is brand new from a homebuilder, or that has already been recently renovated, you are most likely going to pay top dollar. The seller is going to place the price of the home at the higher end of the market because they want to recoup their building and renovation costs.

Keep these facts in mind when you consider purchasing a new home:

- Make sure you have enough money for a down payment before you begin looking for a new house.
- Have a realistic monthly budget that allows you to tithe, save, and then spend the rest.
- Make sure your overall monthly housing expenses do not represent more than 25% of your total monthly budget.
- Do not allow a realtor to show you houses that you cannot afford. It is too easy to fall in love and then be tempted to justify buying a home you simply cannot afford.
- Your first home will most likely not be your forever home.

Do your homework and make intelligent investments in real estate so you can make a profit when you sell your home in the future.

In conclusion, as long as you are an educated, non-emotional buyer with realistic expectations about how much house you can actually afford, definitely consider investing in real estate. A house may be one of the largest purchases you ever make. It can serve several different purposes. Obviously, it will provide shelter for you and your family, which is one of our primary needs as humans. However, it is also a place where precious family memories can be made that will be cherished for many years. A home should be peaceful and a place to rest and recharge your batteries. It can also be a wise investment financially.

Be sure to do your homework before you start house hunting. Be careful not to get emotionally attached to a home in a price range that you simply cannot afford. Pray for guidance before you make any final decisions about the house you will purchase. I do believe if you ask God for wisdom, He will make your path to your new home straight. "Trust in the Lord with all your heart and lean not on your own understanding; in all your ways submit to him, and he will make your paths straight." (Proverbs 3:5-6 NIV)

7

A Penny Saved May Be More Than a Penny Earned

'For I know the plans I have for you,' declares the Lord, 'plans to prosper you and not to harm you, plans to give you hope and a future.'

Jeremiah 29:11 NIV

My friend, Shay, is an African American woman who is quite busy, both personally and professionally. She is a teacher, a single mother to a daughter in kindergarten, and she owns a personal fitness business. Shay recently told me that in her community, people are taught to get a job, cash a paycheck, and go home. They are not taught to take any risks. As a result, Shay sees many people who aren't building wealth. In order to build wealth, a person has to take some risk through investing or starting a business of her own. It takes hard work.

Shay believes that by helping others achieve their goals through fitness, she is helping other people emotionally, physically, and spiritually. Shay enhances and improves the quality of other people's lives. She earns more money counseling and training other people to live a healthier lifestyle than she earns as a teacher. As she helps others achieve their fitness goals, she is simultaneously growing her assets and overall wealth.

Friend, please know that growing wealth and being wise with your assets is Biblical. God blesses those who work hard and make wise decisions. Here is what the Bible has to say about investing wisely in the Book of Matthew:

The Parable of the Bags of Gold

"Again, it will be like a man going on a journey, who called his servants and entrusted his wealth to them. To one he gave five bags of gold, to another two bags, and to another one bag, each according to his ability. Then he went on his journey. The man who had received five bags of gold went at once and put his money to work and gained five bags more. So also, the one with two bags of gold gained two more. But the man who had received one bag went off, dug a hole in the ground and hid his master's money. "After a long time the master of those servants returned and settled accounts with them. The man who had received five bags of gold brought the other five. 'Master,' he said, 'you entrusted me with five bags of gold. See, I have gained five more.' "His master replied, 'Well done, good and faithful servant! You have been faithful with a few things; I will put you in charge of many things. Come and share your master's happiness!' "The man with two bags of gold also came. 'Master,' he said, 'you entrusted me with two bags of gold; see, I have gained two more.' "His master replied, 'Well done, good and faithful servant! You have been faithful with a few things; I will put you in charge of many things. Come and share your master's happiness!' "Then the man who had received one bag of gold came. 'Master,' he said, 'I knew that you are a hard man, harvesting where you have not sown and gathering where you have not scattered seed. So I was afraid and went out and hid your gold in the ground. See, here is what belongs to you.' "His master replied, 'You wicked, lazy servant! So you knew that I harvest where I have not sown and gather where I have not scattered seed? Well then, you should have put my money on deposit with the bankers, so that when I returned I would have received it back with interest. "So take the bag of gold from him and give it to the one who has ten bags. For whoever has will be given more, and they will have an abundance. Whoever does not have, even what they have will be taken from them." (Matthew 25:14-29 NIV)

What do you think this parable is trying to teach us? Quite simply, God wants you to be a wise steward of the money and assets He has given you. What is a wise steward? Let's start with a quick glance at Webster's dictionary:

Steward: A noun, a person employed to manage another's property, esp. a large house or estate; a person whose responsibility it is to take care of something. [11]

So how do we become the kind of person who manages well what God has entrusted to us? Let's make this as simple as possible. Just Remember: **10/10/10/70**.

- **10**: The first 10% of your income should be a tithe and offering to God.
- **10**: The second 10% of you income should be put in a very safe investment or money market account for future liquidity needs.
- **10**: The third 10% of your income should be invested wisely to outpace inflation and grow over time.
- **70**: The remaining 70% of your income should be spent wisely on items you want and/or need.

In this chapter, we'll learn about the third 10% of your monthly income. I want you to consider investing it wisely in order to grow and appreciate over time. Benjamin Franklin is famous for saying, "a penny saved is a penny earned."[12] This is not necessarily true. If you invest wisely, you can actually multiply your money, not just add it. In other words, with wise and strategic investing, a penny saved may turn unto five pennies. There are many different instruments, or products, available today to help grow your assets with interest. If you invest in the following types of investments, you can benefit from compound interest:

- Money market cash accounts
- Bank Certificates of Deposit (often referred to as CDs)
- Bonds
- Annuities

Compound interest is interest added to the principal of a deposit, or loan, so that the added interest also earns interest from then on. This addition of interest to the principal is called *compounding*. A bank account may have its interest compounded every year. For example, an account with $1,000.00 of initial principal and 5% interest per year would have a balance of $1,050.00 at the end of the first year, $1,102.50 at the end of the second year, $1,157.62 at the end of the third year, and so on. In other words, the harder your money works, the less you have to work.

There is a little known calculation you can perform in personal finance to determine how many years it will take to double your money. It is called *The Rule of 72*. You divide 72 by the annual interest rate you are receiving on your investment and it will tell you how long it will take to double your money. For example, if I invest $100,000 in a money market account earning 1% per year, it will take me 72 years (72/1=72) to double my money. On the other hand, if I invest $100,000 in a mutual fund earning 8% per year, it will only take me nine years to double my investment and have $200,000 (72/8=9).

Please remember that it takes time for money to grow. In a world bent on quick money, we must remember this principle. Many people have lost their entire savings because they trusted in a get-rich-quick scheme. Be very cautious if a broker promises an extremely high rate of return that is obviously unrealistic. Besides compound interest, you can also grow your investments by capital appreciation. The following investments increase in value as the underlying investment, or capital, appreciates in value:

- Stocks
- Mutual funds containing stock
- Tangible Real Estate such as a home or office building
- REIT's (Real Estate Investment Trusts) that are portfolios of commercial real estate that investors can purchase shares of

Friend, if you truly are an investor, you are not putting money in the lottery or gambling. Investors take a long-term approach to growing their wealth. They plant the seed, then water the seed, and then watch the tree grow over time. It is a process. This is called investing, and not speculation.

A speculator, as opposed to an investor, does not take into account the overall risk of her portfolio. She is trying to "hit it big" by investing in one new idea or product. Tech companies offering brand new technology are examples of speculative investments. The company does not have a track record but the product is supposed to be the next big thing. Speculators take large risks in the hope of making quick money. I do not advise you to make speculative investments unless the money you are investing truly is fun money. In other words, if you lost every single penny you made in a speculative investment, you and your family would not suffer at all financially.

An important question to consider is, "Am I an investor or a speculator?" Investors save and invest systematically every month. They focus on buying good solid investments that are allocated to a well-diversified portfolio. They do not get emotional about daily movements in the stock market indexes. Their investment approach is often referred to as a "buy and hold" strategy. Another very important quality of a good investor is to have assets that are non-correlated to one another. Non-correlated assets do not increase or decrease at the same time. For example, stocks and bonds do not usually both increase or decrease at the same time. The overall goal with investing is to grow your assets, while also managing your investment risk.

One way to take volatility out of your investment portfolio is the use of Dollar Cost Averaging. According to *Investopedia*, the following is a simple, clear definition of the strategy:

> Dollar-Cost Averaging is the technique of buying a fixed dollar amount of a particular investment on a regular schedule, regardless of the share price. More shares are purchased when prices are low, and fewer shares are bought when prices are high. Eventually, the average cost per share of the security will become smaller and smaller. Dollar-cost averaging lessens the risk of investing a large amount in a single investment at the wrong time. For example, you decide to purchase $100 worth of XYZ each month for three months. In January, XYZ is worth $33, so you buy three shares. In February, XYZ is worth $25, so you buy four additional shares. Finally, in March, XYZ is worth $20, so you buy five shares. In total, you purchased 12 shares for an average price of approximately $25 each.[13]

Please remember, dollar cost averaging cannot protect against loss in a generally declining market. Past performance is not a guarantee of future results. If you ever have an advisor guarantee you anything, be very skeptical. This is why it is so important to balance your risk when you invest money. You do not want to keep your money under a mattress to avoid any volatility, but you also want to be prudent about your investments.

The word *risk* has a negative sound to it. However, if we break risk down into the components of what it really stands for in terms of investing, it begins to be a little more manageable. I promise you that you will be better equipped to manage your money effectively if you understand the different types of risk. Long-term investing, or the buy and hold strategy, as well as diversification, are some of the most effective strategies you can use to help manage investment risk. Unfortunately, there are no full proof guarantees against investment loss. Let me explain the different types of investment risk...

Inflation Risk
Risk from inflation is the danger that inflation will reduce your purchasing power and the returns from your investments. If your savings and investments are failing to outpace inflation, you might consider investing in growth-oriented alternatives such as stocks, stock mutual funds, variable annuities, or other vehicles.

Interest Rate Risk
A bond is simply an 'IOU' in which an investor agrees to loan money to a company or government in exchange for a predetermined interest rate for a pre-determined length of time.[14] Bonds and other fixed-income investments tend to be sensitive to changes in interest rates. When interest rates rise, the value of these investments falls. After all, why would someone pay full price for your bond at 3% when new bonds are being issued at 5%? The opposite is also true. When interest rates fall, existing bonds increase in value.

Economic Risk
When the economy experiences a downturn, the earnings capabilities of most firms are threatened. While some industries and companies adjust to downturns in the economy very well, others such as large industrial firms take longer to react.

Market Risk
A "security" is a catch-all term for many kinds of investments. When a market experiences a downturn, it tends to pull down most of its securities with it. Afterward, the affected securities will recover at rates more closely related to their fundamental strength. Market risk affects almost all types of investments, including stocks, bonds, real estate, and others. Historically, long-term investing has been a way to minimize the effects of market risk.

Specific Risk
Events may occur that only affect a specific company or industry. For example, the death of a young company's president may

cause the value of the company's stock to drop. It's almost impossible to pinpoint all these influences, but diversifying your investments could help manage the effects of specific risks.

I can speak from experience that managing risk is crucial to weathering the ups and downs of the stock market. Not only do I manage my family's money, but I am also responsible for my clients' investment accounts that I manage as their financial advisor. I know intellectually that I must invest in stocks, or equities, to allow my investments to grow more than inflation over the long term. As a result, I know there will also be some volatility over time.

You may be surprised to hear this, but the ups and downs in my clients' accounts affect me more emotionally that the volatility in my own investment accounts. That is why I always make sure that the portfolios I manage are extremely well diversified. I do not speculate on anything. I feel an extreme responsibility to protect and grow my client's wealth. I consider it an honor and a compliment that someone has entrusted me with their money. If I do not practice what I preach by utilizing both diversification and asset allocation tools when selecting investments, I wouldn't be able to sleep at night. I would be on a constant roller coaster of emotion as the Dow Jones Industrial Average or the S&P500 Index increased, or decreased, each day.

You may be asking yourself right about now, "What really is the Dow Jones Industrial Average, or DOW, as it is frequently referred to? What is the S&P 500 index? What Index do they use to measure the performance of bonds?" Let me answer these questions for you.

The Dow Jones Industrial Average (DJIA) is a price-weighted average of ONLY 30 significant stocks traded on the New York Stock Exchange and the DASDAQ. Charles Dow originally invented the DJIA back in 1896. Often referred to as "the Dow," the DJIA is one of the oldest and single most watched indexes in the world. The DJIA includes companies like General Electric, Disney, Exxon and Microsoft. When the TV networks say, "the market is up today," they are generally referring to the Dow Jones Industrial Average.

The S&P 500 Index contains 500 stocks chosen for market size, liquidity and industry grouping, among other factors. The S&P 500 index is designed to be a leading indicator of U.S. stocks. The purpose of the index is to reflect the risk/return characteristics of the large cap universe of stocks. Companies included in this index are selected by members of the S&P Index Committee, a team of analysts and economists at Standard & Poor's. The S&P 500 is a market value weighted index. Each stock's weight is proportionate to its market value.

The S&P 500 is one of the most commonly used benchmarks for the overall U.S. stock market. The Dow Jones Industrial Average (DJIA) was at one time the most renowned index for U.S. stocks, but because the DJIA contains only 30 companies, most people agree that the S&P 500 is a better representation of the U.S. market. In fact, many consider it to be the definition of the market.

The Lehman Aggregate Bond Index is an index used by bond funds as a benchmark to measure relative performance of different types of securities. The index includes government securities, mortgage-backed securities, asset-backed securities, and corporate securities. The maturities of the bonds in the index are more than one year.

If you are invested in a diversified portfolio, and *not* an index mutual fund that tracks any of these indexes, then you do not need to worry about the performance of these indexes on a daily basis. I never invest my money, or any of my client's money, solely in an index. As a result, the investment accounts will not mimic these indexes. They will not go up as much, or down as much, as either of these indexes fluctuate and change. This is an important concept to remember, especially if you listen to news channels on a frequent basis that sensationalize changes in the stock market indexes. You may have also heard people say that investing is really easy. "Just buy yourself a good index mutual fund and let your money ride. Don't worry about it." You hear this when the stock market is performing well. Everyone is a stockbroker in bull markets. Diversification and asset allocation techniques usually only get the credit they deserve in Bear markets, or stock market corrections. We will discuss these strategies in more detail in Chapter 8. When you invest money in order to generate interest income, capital appreciation, or hopefully both, you are seeking what is known as passive income. Passive income is very important in the pursuit of financial freedom. Passive income is also known as "unearned income." It is an income stream that you receive on a regular basis, with little effort required to maintain it. This is a very key component to building wealth. Someone, or something, has to generate income to support you and your family. Wouldn't you rather your money work harder so you do not have to? Another term for passive income that I like is "mailbox money." Some people think that passive income is about getting something for nothing. Passive income is not a "get rich quick" scheme. There is still work involved initially to create the income stream.

Invest in Dividend Yielding Stocks

Dividend yielding stocks are purchased in order to provide the investor with an income stream. "Dividend yield" is a calculation used to determine how much income the investor will receive for each dollar invested. Owning dividend-yielding stocks is definitely one of the most common ways to generate a passive income stream.

Many novices to the stock market jump in without investigating the financial statements of the company that is issuing the stock. This can be risky. Please watch out for "dividend traps." If a corporation offers a dividend yield, or income stream, equal to 10 percent or more annually, it's probably a pretty risky investment.

Invest in Rental Properties

This is an effective and time-honored way of earning passive income. However, it requires more work than people might expect. You have to do your due diligence on the real estate properties you consider purchasing in order to make a wise investment. If you want to earn passive income from a rental property, you must analyze the following investment factors:

- The return on investment
- The purchase price of the property
- The costs and expenses of properly maintaining the property
- Whether or not there is a rental market for your home
- The financial risks of owning the property

Example: Your personal goal is to earn $24,000 a year in rental income. You have a mortgage on the property that requires a $1,500 monthly payment. Your rental property also requires an additional $300 a month in taxes and other expenses to maintain the property. In order to reach your goal of $24,000 of passive income per year, (average of $2,000 per month), you will need to charge at least $3,800 in rent each month. Now the question becomes one of risk: Is there a market for your property? What if you get a deadbeat tenant? Will your tenant damage the property? All of these factors could result in a sizable deduction in your passive income *and* your underlying investment in real estate.

Selling Information Products
Some people fantasize about creating passive income by creating and selling an information product, such as an ebook, CD, or DVD. They picture themselves sitting back while cash from the sales of these products just rolls in. This is often touted among Internet marketing gurus as an easy, surefire way to create a passive-income stream. But while information products can eventually yield an excellent stream, creating information products is hardly a passive activity. It takes a large amount of time, energy, and creativity to create the product. Most importantly, the product has to be some thing that people are willing to pay money for.

Affiliate Marketing
Website owners or bloggers promote a third party's product by including a link to the product on their site. If a visitor clicks

on the link and makes a purchase from the third party, the site owner receives a commission, generally around 15 to 20 percent. Affiliate marketing is considered passive because, in theory, you can earn money just by adding the link to your website. In reality, you have to find a way to attract readers to your site, click on the link, and buy something. It is an on-going marketing project.

Peer-to-Peer (P2P) Lending

This is a new way of creating passive income. A person, rather than a bank, acts as a lender in order to earn returns as high as 8 to 12 percent. A P2P loan is a personal loan facilitated through a third-party intermediary, such as www.Prosper.com, or www.LendingClub.com. The loans are unsecured so a lender must be aware of the risk of default. It is wise to diversify a lending portfolio by investing smaller amounts over multiple loans. The time it takes to master the metrics is just one of the reasons that P2P lending isn't entirely passive. Since you're investing in multiple loans, you really need to pay close attention to payments received and other book keeping requirements.

I want to encourage you to invest your money. You have to decide which strategy, or combination of strategies is right for your particular situation. One size does not fit all. As you grow your wealth through savings and investments, opportunities will most likely increase in your life. Money is a tool to be used wisely. It is a good thing. Steve Siebold wrote a book called, *How Rich People Think*. According to Mr. Siebold, "The average family unconsciously passes down the same limiting beliefs they were taught about money from generation to generation. These are the beliefs that have kept families at the same level of financial success for dozens, if not hundreds, of years. Wealthy people, on the other hand, not only teach their kids smart money habits, but they teach them wealth is possible for anyone who thinks big enough. They educate their kids on how to make money by solving problems and enhancing the quality of other people's lives. This way the child learns to see money as a positive, productive force for good."[15]

Friend, all of your money belongs to God. He wants you to use it wisely, grow it, and bless others as a result. If you will change your focus to see money as a tool to be used for good, it may radically change your life. I want to empower you to think boldly and outside of the box about investing your most precious commodity, your time. It is a finite resource. Remember my friend Shay whenever you start to think that you cannot do hard things. Consider investing your money. Consider starting your own business. You can never get fired if you are your own boss. Pray about it and see how God leads you. I promise you that He already has a great plan for you. He is just patiently waiting for you to ask and seek Him regarding what your next step in life should be with investing and growing your assets.

8

Do Not Put All of Your Eggs in One Basket

For you created my inmost being; you knit me together in my mother's womb. I praise you because I am fearfully and wonderfully made; your works are wonderful, I know that full well. My frame was not hidden from you when I was made in the secret place, when I was woven together in the depths of the earth. Your eyes saw my unformed body; all the days ordained for me were written in your book before one of them came to be.

Psalms 139:13-16 NIV

Fertility treatments are used to help a woman conceive a baby who is having trouble getting pregnant on her own. It is a nerve-racking process because the stakes are very high. The journey is often an emotional roller coaster. The process is very expensive and it may determine the future for a couple desperately wanting to have a baby and start a family. Sometimes fertility treatments are successful and sometimes they are not. There are no guarantees. The process is entirely based on a game of odds.

In my particular case, I desperately wanted another child and a sibling for my daughter. However, due to some significant health challenges that I had endured both before and after the birth of my daughter, I was advised not to carry a baby again myself. It was just too risky. After many years of prayer, my husband and I chose to try to have a baby via surrogacy. The first step was to harvest my eggs. In order to do so, I had to take some very strong prescription drugs with many negative side effects to stimulate my ovaries to produce as many eggs as possible. Then, I had to go to the fertility doctor's office to have a blood draw to measure my egg production, *every single day*. It was miserable. I had to keep reminding myself that this process was temporary and it would all be worth it when we met our new baby very soon. Finally, the day arrived when they knew that I was at "maximum capacity" for creating eggs and it was time to have them surgically removed. This is called the "egg retrieval." The timing of the egg retrieval is based on scientific calculations that will supposedly give you the highest success rate.

After my egg retrieval, I sighed a big sigh of relief because at least my part was done. I could stop taking the horrible fertility drugs that have so many side effects and try to get my body back to normal.

We had to wait a certain number of days after they created our embryos in the lab before they could be transferred surgically to the surrogate mother's uterus. They were waiting for the best possible time in her monthly cycle so she would have the highest probability of getting pregnant. Our embryologist told us that he was able to create and keep alive seven embryos. Most people that go through the process of harvesting their eggs end up with many more embryos than we did. This put even more pressure on everyone. They recommended that we use our two best embryos for the first embryo transfer surgery.

I will never forget the day of the embryo transfer surgery. The surrogate mother and her husband were there along with my husband and myself. The fertility doctor was in rare form. Embryo transfer day is like his Super Bowl. You could tell he particularly loved helping couples have a baby that had challenges doing so on their own. After the surgery, there was simply MORE WAITING. It would be about two weeks before we would know if our surrogate mother was pregnant with our baby or maybe even BABIES. Meanwhile, the embryologist was closely monitoring our other embryos in his laboratory. He would continue to take care of them for about a week until he determined the best time to freeze them. He finally called the following Friday night. I remember where I was. I was washing dishes at the kitchen sink. By Friday, we only had three embryos left that had survived. However, he told me that the three remaining embryos were "rock stars" and that he would be freezing them the following morning to be used in case our surrogate mother did not get pregnant the first time.

The phone rang again pretty early on Saturday morning and it was the embryologist again. I knew he would be calling to confirm that our embryos were now frozen. When he began to talk that morning, his voice sounded a bit shaky. I could not figure out why he was acting like he was preparing me for bad news. We had just talked about twelve hours earlier. "Emily, I am so sorry but none of the three remaining healthy embryos survived through the night. I do not know what happened or why they did not make it. Unfortunately, we have nothing left to freeze. This is extremely unusual. The odds of this happening are very rare. I sincerely hope that the two embryos we transferred last week to your surrogate mother have implanted because that is all you have left."

All of our eggs were now in one basket. I continued to pray, as I had for days, that our surrogate mother was already in fact pregnant with our child or children. We had no choice but to continue to wait. Would it be one baby or two babies? Oh I hoped it would be twins. I could hardly wait for the phone call that I hoped and prayed would change our family's future forever. I imagined how fun it was going to be to tell our story and how God had brought me through so many health challenges. Now he would be giving us the ultimate gift of a baby and a sibling for our daughter. I just knew that this was going to bring so much Glory to God. I could not wait!

Finally, the phone rang. I looked at it twice before I answered the phone. This was it. Here we go. Holding my breath, I said, 'Hello." My surrogate mother's voice was on the other end of the telephone. Finally she gave me the news we had all been waiting for. "Emily, I am so sorry but I just found out that I am in fact not pregnant." I was stunned. I got off the phone, and fell to my knees and sobbed. I was devastated. How could God have let us spend all of this money and time and energy for it to all fall apart? I put my life at risk taking the high dosages of fertility medications all for nothing. We prayed for two years before we moved forward. We continually asked God to shut the door if this was not the right path for us. We did not move forward with the next step until my husband and I both were in agreement. Then I suddenly remembered that I would now have to tell everyone that it did not work out. There would not be a new baby today and there would not be another baby EVER. We had put all of our eggs in one basket and it did not work out.

I often feel like an embryologist when I am managing someone's "nest egg" or investment portfolio. Just like expectant parents want a healthy baby the very first time they try to get pregnant, investors are impatient and want very high investment returns immediately. In addition, they may or may not have any risk tolerance. They want their money managers to be magicians. I have news for you. We are not.

Some investors think I have failed if the assets in their portfolio temporarily decrease in value. They call me in a panic and they want to bail out of the market. This is the worst mistake I see investors make. They get extremely worried as soon as their investment portfolio experiences any volatility. What they do not understand is the process is a marathon and not a sprint.

A money manager really earns their stripes when the stock market is going down and not up. It is easy to make money when the stock market is flying high in a bull market. In a bull market share prices of stocks are rising and expected to continue to rise as well. I often joke, "During bull markets, I feel like I can throw things on a dart board and make money, and everyone thinks I'm a hero." I am not a hero. I am just doing my job.

As money managers, we are graded based on benchmarks. As we discussed in Chapter 7, we normally use the S&P 500 Index as a benchmark for a stock, or equity, portfolio. We also use the Lehman Aggregate Bond Index as a benchmark for a bond portfolio. An 80/20 portfolio would only be appropriate for someone in her 20s that has at least 30 to 40 years to ride out the volatility over time. An 80/20 portfolio allocates 80% of its funds to the stock market or equities and 20% to the bond market or fixed income. This is called asset allocation. If my client's portfolio increases in value by 8% while the S&P 500 stock index rises by 14%, she might be angry and think I am doing a poor job of managing her money.

I often have to reiterate to new investors that they are not 100% invested in the stock market. That would be foolish. If I am doing my job, my client's investment accounts will never increase in value as much as the stock market index increases on any single day, and it will *never* decrease in value as much as the stock market tumbles on any one bad day. A portion of their money is invested in the stock market, and a portion is invested in more conservative, or fixed income, investments. This is done purposefully and strategically to give investors upside potential with downside protection. Together, before I ever invest any money, my clients and I both agree upon the best asset mix for their individual account. This strategy is called Asset Allocation. We make this decision based on the following criteria:

- How much of their overall net worth are we investing?
- The client's age
- Their individual risk tolerance
- Time frame for investing

According to *Investopedia*, the definition of Asset Allocation is: "The relative percentages of core asset classes in a portfolio such as equities, fixed income and cash, along with real estate and international holdings, found within a mutual fund, exchange-traded fund or other portfolio. Further breakdowns are sometimes made within the asset classes into growth stocks, value stocks, market capitalizations (small, medium, large) and various types of fixed income such as government bonds, corporate bonds and municipal bonds. Asset class breakdowns are calculated by dividing the market value of a particular asset class's holdings by the total fund or portfolio assets."[16]

Another key to successful investing is managing risk

while maintaining the potential for adequate returns on your investments. One of the most effective ways to help manage your investment risk is to diversify the assets in your overall portfolio. The purpose of diversification is to manage risk by spreading your money across a variety of investments such as: stocks, bonds, real estate, commodities, and cash alternatives. However, please remember that diversification does not guarantee a profit or protect against loss.

The main philosophy behind diversification is really quite simple: "Don't put all of your eggs in one basket." As I mentioned earlier, an embryologist carefully watches all of a mother's embryos in his laboratory to determine which embryos, out of all that were created, will have the highest probability of implanting in her uterus and forming a healthy baby. The embryologist never gives the mother any guarantees. He just makes the most educated recommendation he can based on years of training and experience. As investment managers, we also are spreading out risk in our client's portfolios among different investment categories, as well as over several different industries and even geographic regions. Diversification can help offset a loss in any one investment.

The power of diversification will most likely help smooth out your total investment returns over time. As one investment increases, it may offset the decreases in another. This will allow your portfolio to ride out market fluctuations, providing a more steady performance under various economic conditions. By potentially reducing the impact of market ups and downs, diversification could go far in enhancing your comfort level with investing.

Diversification is one of the main reasons why mutual funds may be attractive to both experienced and novice investors. Many non-institutional investors have a limited investment budget and may find it challenging to construct a portfolio that is sufficiently diversified. For a modest initial investment, you can purchase shares in a diversified portfolio of securities called a mutual fund. The funds offer investors built-in diversification. Depending on the objectives of the mutual fund, it may contain a variety of stocks, bonds, and cash vehicles, or a combination of them.

It is interesting to me that diversification is part of Modern Portfolio Theory. However, it is discussed in the Bible that was written thousands of years ago. "Invest in seven ventures, yes, in eight; you do not know what disaster may come upon the land." (Ecclesiastes 11:2 NIV) This is the definition of diversification of assets. We can make wise assessments of market conditions, but nobody knows for certain what the future holds. If a financial advisor or money manager ever guarantees you anything, please be skeptical. You really need to spread your assets out among a variety of asset classes. Then you will not be overexposed to any particular investment or asset class. Money managers do not have a crystal ball. No one does.

Whether you are investing in mutual funds, self-directing your own combination of stocks, bonds, and other investment vehicles, or working with a money manager, it is wise to understand the importance of asset allocation and diversifying the assets inside of your accounts. The value of individual stocks, bonds, and mutual funds will fluctuate over time depending upon market conditions. Just make sure you are not overly exposed to any one single stock or investment. I want to remind you again that you are not in control. Investing is simply the management of odds.

I am happy to report that the end of our family's story was not over after we were unable to have a baby via surrogacy.

Friend, it is so easy to be thankful and trust God during the good and fruitful times in your life. It is definitely not a natural response to choose to trust God when you are in pain. You have to choose to trust Him even though you do not like what happened. You also have to choose to believe with certainty, that eventually His plan will be revealed to you. That plan may or may not be revealed to you this side of heaven, but eventually you will know and have closure. I want to encourage you to cling to God's Word during trials in your life. You need His truth to dominate your thoughts, so that your faith is stronger than your fear and your pain. Nothing else will ever bring true healing.

One morning in March of 2010, my husband proceeded to

tell me that he just had a very vivid dream. "In my dream, you were healthy and pregnant and the baby was going to be due at Thanksgiving time this year." I politely asked my husband not to bring up the subject of me being pregnant again. It still was an extremely sensitive issue. However, he respectfully told me that he felt that this dream was more than "just a dream." He said, "I know that it sounds crazy, but it felt more like a vision from God." He kept saying that he felt like God had given him this dream so that he would feel at peace and not be worried about my health or the baby's health if I became pregnant. He believed that the dream was God's way of telling him that everything was going to turn out well.

According to my physician, there was no way that I could be pregnant. My body had been through too much trauma in years past and my eggs were not viable. That is why none of our embryos survived long enough to be frozen, and the two embryos transferred to my surrogate mother's uterus did not implant, and allow her to get pregnant. However, just in case, I drove 90 miles per hour to the local drugstore and bought three new pregnancy tests. I made sure a different manufacturer made each one, so we could not possibly get two false positives. Remember, I am in the profession of managing odds. I was not going to take any chances. I took every single one of those new pregnancy tests. Each one said the exact same thing. I was going to have a baby. I was *truly* shocked. Even more amazing, the baby was due the following November at Thanksgiving time, just as my husband had dreamed about.

All I could think was, "How is this even possible? The doctor said it was absolutely not possible." And then I remembered that I do not worship a God of odds! Now He would be glorified in the way He deserved to be honored and worshipped. There was no scientist that could take credit for the conception of this baby in a laboratory. This baby was conceived in such a way to show that God alone is in fact in control of the universe. There is no amount of money, advances in science, or statistics that can explain this miracle.

God had a greater plan for us all along. He asked us to go down the journey of surrogacy for a reason. It allowed me to lay down my "all-consuming" desire to have a baby at the foot of the cross. He made sure the world knew that science was not responsible for the conception of this child. It was God.

Since God had obviously given my husband the vision that I was pregnant, I immediately asked him if it was a boy or a girl. He laughed and said that God did not reveal that detail. "Darn!" I thought. I would really like to know so I can start planning. He laughingly said, "Some things and some people never change."

9

My Kids Want to Go to College. Now What?

*Instruct the wise and they will be wiser still;
teach the righteous and
they will add to their learning.*

Proverbs 9:9 NIV

I recently had the opportunity to visit with a group of twelve women to get their perspective on paying for college for their children. I asked each person if they had started saving for college for their children, and what they planned to provide, if possible, for their kids. I really liked what my friend Mary Annelle had to share. Interestingly enough, Mary Annelle was one of my college roommates at Texas A&M University. It seems very surreal that we are now discussing how we will pay for college for our own children. The common thread among the women I interviewed is that they all value education and believe it is a gift. I could not agree more.

Mary Annelle and her husband, Bryan, have always been very purposeful with financial planning. Bryan is a lawyer and also has an M.B.A. He is quite analytical. Mary Annelle stays home with their four children and does a great job managing her household budget and all of the responsibilities of caring for four children, ages: 12, 10, 7 and 5. As a couple, Mary Annelle and Bryan feel that it is their responsibility to pay for college for their four children. However, it is not, "Whatever they want, wherever they want to go." They are budgeting to pay for four years of tuition at a public, state school for each of their children. If any of their children wish to go out of state or to a private university, they will have to supplement the cost of their education with student loans, scholarships, or income they generate while working and going to school.

Mary Annelle and Bryan are already having discussions with their children about college. They want to let their kids know early in life what to expect from them financially as parents. There will be no surprises when their kids are old enough to start applying to college. Mary Annelle and Bryan have been saving for each child's education with 529 College Savings plans. God willing, they will be prepared financially to pay for the expenses of college for all four children if they continue with the savings plans they have already established. Most importantly, they have not sacrificed their own retirement savings. They agree that it is not an option to consider using their retirement savings to supplement the cost of a private, or out of state university, in the future for one of their children.

The best part about proactive financial planning for both college savings needs for your children, and retirement, is that it takes any guessing and emotion out of the financial decisions that must be made over time. Everyone's expectations are managed early on. Mary Annelle and Bryan are great examples of being proactive, rather than reactive, with their financial decisions.

One of the questions that keep many parents up at night is the following: What is the best way to save for my child's college education? I have good news for you. There are now more tax credits and savings vehicles specifically for college expenses than ever before. The best time to start saving for your children's college expenses is now. The earlier you start saving, the more likely your child will have the opportunity to attend college without a large financial burden to either one of you.

It is very important to find a balance between saving for college education costs for your children, while also continuing to save for your own retirement. Keep the following facts in mind when thinking about college savings needs for your children, while also saving for your own retirement years:

- Be sure to take full advantage of any employer sponsored retirement plans such as a 401k, or 403b tax sheltered annuity, before you allocate any more of your discretionary income to college savings accounts.
- Company sponsored retirement plans offer special tax advantages and often provide matching contributions from employers. If you do not participate in your company's retirement plan, you may be paying more federal income taxes than necessary. In addition, you could be leaving free money on the table if your employer provides matching contributions to your retirement plan.
- Your retirement assets are not taken into account when your child applies for Federal Financial Aid for college.
- Your IRA accounts can be used as secondary funding sources to help pay for college expenses for your children. You are allowed to take funds out of a Traditional IRA, or Roth IRA, without paying a 10% early withdrawal penalty, if the funds are used to pay for qualified education expenses.
- The only way you can use funds in your 401k plan to help pay for college for your children is to take a loan, up to a maximum of $50,000. Unlike withdrawals from an IRA to pay for college expenses, any loan taken from a 401k plan must be paid back.
- Always remember that if you use some of your own retirement accounts to pay for your children's college expenses today, the funds might not be there for you when you need them in retirement. You risk paying for college for your kids now only to be a burden to them later in life.

I want to teach you how to afford to pay for college for your children. It can be done. The first step is to do research to determine how much it could potentially cost to send your child to college. The following website: www.savingforcollege.com has lots of valuable resources for parents and students. In addition, the website has a great college savings calculator. If you want to determine now approximately how much it will cost to send your child to college in the future, you will be asked to enter the following variables in the online savings calculator:

- The age of your child
- How much money has already been saved
- Type of college or university you are wiling to pay for such as: local community college, a state university, an out of state university, or a private university

The calculator will then estimate the future education costs for your child. Please remember, just like any other projection, the calculations are based on variables that may change over time.

There are multiple ways for your children to receive a college education. Try to keep an open mind when considering various options for educating your children. One way to save a considerable amount of money on tuition, as well as other fees and expenses, is to have your child attend a local community college for the first two years of college. You will save even more money if your child can continue to live at home, while attending community college. Then neither the child nor the parent will have to pay rent for an apartment, or the cost of room and board in a dormitory.

Another idea to consider is an in-state public university in the state in which you currently live. Tuition and fees for public universities are considerably more affordable than private universities, or out-of-state public universities. You will have to decide which type of school is best for your child, and affordable for your family. I recommend going to visit some colleges and universities way before your child plans to actually attend college. The decision will be much less emotional and you will be able to make a well-informed decision as a family.

The steady rise in the cost of a college education has slowed somewhat during the past two years. At public four-year schools, the average inflation-adjusted cost of tuition, fees, room, and board increased just 1.2% in the 2013–2014 academic year, and 1.0% in 2014–2015. At private universities, the increases were 1.8% and 1.6%, respectively. That's good news for families with current or future students. But even so, college is expensive[17].

Despite the cost, higher education is still a valuable investment. College graduates not only earn more than non-graduates, but also tend to be healthier, more satisfied with their jobs and more likely to remain employed during touch economic times. A strategic savings plan could be a key step toward providing your student with the many benefits of a college diploma.

Please make sure you do not overlook the opportunity for scholarships and grant money to offset the cost of your child's college expenses. In certain cases, the only way a child will be able to attend college is through student loans. There is no shame in that; it is actually quite common. However, if your child receives scholarship or grant money, they will never have to pay that money back after graduation. It is well worth the effort to seek out and apply for federal grants and private scholarships.

Let's discuss the pros and cons of different ways to save for your children's future education costs. I have compiled the following information from a trusted resource, Emerald Connect.[18]

State or College Sponsored Plan

State or college-sponsored programs are designed to help families save for future higher-education expenses. These plans have been available since 1996, but legislation passed in December 2014 provided additional investment flexibility. These changes should be welcome to parents and grandparents who utilize these plans to save for their children or grandchildren's college education.

The funds in a college savings plan accumulate on a tax-deferred basis and can be withdrawn free of federal income tax when used for qualified education expenses at accredited post-secondary schools, such as colleges, universities, community colleges, and certain technical schools. Qualified expenses include tuition, fees, room and board, books, and supplies. theplans feature high contribution limits (set by each state), and there are no income restrictions for donors.

The tax implications of a college savings plan should be discussed with your legal and/or tax advisors because they can vary significantly from state to state. Most states offer their own college savings programs, which may provide advantages and benefits exclusively for their residents and taxpayers.

Before investing in a college savings plan, be sure to consider the investment objectives, risks, charges, and expenses carefully.

Universal Life Insurance

Universal life insurance policies build cash value through regular premiums and grow at competitive rates. The policies carry a death benefit. In addition to providing cash to your heirs in the event of your death, money can be withdrawn from these contracts through policy loans, often at no interest. The withdrawals may reduce the policy's death benefit but you are free to use the funds inside the policy however you wish. Some families are using life insurance for more than one financial goal. They are using some of the cash that grows tax deferred to pay for college expenses for their children. The insurance policy protects their family in the event of death, but it also is a savings vehicle with tax advantages, and protection from creditors and legal suits.

Mutual Funds

As you learned in the last chapter, an investment company establishes mutual funds by pooling the monies of many different investors and then investing that money in a diversified portfolio of securities. These securities are selected to meet the specific goals of the fund. The value of mutual fund shares fluctuates with market conditions so that, when sold, shares may be worth more or less than their original cost. Some families are choosing to use mutual funds to help save for college expenses, because there is more flexibility with how to use the funds in the future. Some families earmark their mutual funds for college expenses in the future for their kids, but also use them as a safety net if the family has an emergency or urgent liquidity need.

While I met with the women in my focus group, who were discussing the subject of saving for college for their children, one person mentioned putting parameters on their child's performance during college. How this works: You have them sign a contract before they go to college if you are paying for their tuition. Therefore, there is open communication and there are no surprises. Some great parameters to consider for your own children are the following:

- Your child must maintain a 3.0 GPA or higher for you to continue to pay for their tuition while they attend college.
- If your child fails a course, the child is responsible for paying the parents back for the tuition of the course they failed.
- The child must finish school in four years. They know when they start their freshmen year at college that you will not pay for more than four years of school. Obviously, if there are extenuating circumstances you can adjust this over time. However, manage your child's expectations *before* they start college so they do not think they are on an unlimited gravy train.
- Some parents will only pay for tuition, but not for room and board. This encourages a child to choose a local school so they can live at home and save considerable money on their living expenses.

The best way to meet your future school obligations and savings needs is little by little over time. Proverbs 13:11 reminds us that, "Dishonest money dwindles away, but whoever gathers money little by little makes it grow." I encourage you to do your research and come up with a realistic budget for the cost of educating your children. Use the online calculator I mentioned previously at www.savingforcollege.com to determine how much you need to start saving today to meet your goals. I strongly believe that education is a valuable gift to give to your children and/or grandchildren. Education is a legacy and it is one of the greatest equalizers in our society. It teaches an individual to think and analyze. It is a means to freedom and independence rather than dependence. Maimonides was a famous Spanish Philosopher born on March 30, 1135. He is famous for teaching the following: *Give a man a fish and you feed him for a day; teach a man to fish and you feed him for a lifetime.*[19] Isn't it interesting that nothing has changed in almost 1,000 years?

10

Is Your Life Insured?

Anyone who does not provide for their relatives, and especially for their own household, has denied the faith and is worse than an unbeliever.

1 Timothy 5:8 NIV

This past year, my husband's beloved grandmother passed away at the age of 87. She had suffered with Alzheimer's disease for several years, so her body began to fail her rapidly. She had lived a very fruitful life, and it was a blessing that now she was with her Savior. She had a close, personal relationship with Jesus throughout her entire life. Her family and friends were at peace knowing that she would spend eternity with her Heavenly Father. There was no doubt or fear associated with death for her. She knew beyond a shadow of a doubt that her eternal life was, in fact, insured.

I volunteered to write her eulogy after she passed away last December. I wanted to help my family celebrate her life. My plan was that the pastor who would officiate her funeral would read the eulogy that I had written. Much to my surprise, he asked me to deliver the eulogy that I had written. Now that was not the deal. That was *way* out of my comfort zone.

Honestly, I absolutely did not want to do it. I wanted to give lots of excuses as to why it was just not possible. However, I had no legitimate reason except that I was scared to deliver an emotional eulogy in front of a large crowd. I am a financial advisor by trade. Discussing graphs and charts, or counseling couples on how to obtain financial freedom is where my comfort zone lies. Giving eulogies at funerals is not exactly my wheelhouse. What if I cried? Or worse, what if I embarrassed my family or myself? It felt too raw. It made me feel way too vulnerable. After much prayer, I realized that it all boiled down to fear. That was the only thing holding me back. Suddenly, I remembered a very important scripture. "For God has not given us the spirit of fear; but of power, and of love, and of a sound mind." (2 Timothy 1:7 NIV)

Have you ever been so daunted by the thought of taking a risk that you felt completely overwhelmed? Fear can cripple you if you let it dominate your thoughts and your emotions. I have learned that when I choose faith instead of fear as my guiding light, I will be stretched beyond my safe comfort zone. This is exactly when true heart change takes place and real growth begins.

While I was deciding whether or not I was going to trust God to help me deliver the eulogy, I started thinking about my daughter. How would I encourage her if she faced a difficult situation, and she was scared or afraid? Then it all became very clear. It was an honor to be asked to deliver the eulogy and I would accept the invitation. We teach our children the most by our actions and not our words. When it is all said and done, our children will catch more things that we actually did than words or lectures that we teach. I really like what Jen Hatmaker recently said during an interview with *Guideposts* magazine, "Well done will make much more of an impact on our kids than well said."[20] I wanted my daughter to know that I was nervous, but I also had faith that God would equip me. I want my daughter to know that she can trust Him above all else when she needs strength to carry out her calling.

I want that to be the gift that I share with you as well, my friend. When you are facing a challenging situation, you can pray to a God who will always listen. He will never leave you or forsake you, according to Hebrews 13:5. Most importantly, He will never hurt you or disappoint you. Please know for certain that you can boldly ask God to give you strength and poise to live out your life's purpose.

What would you do today if you finally said yes to Jesus and decided to put your faith in Him? What would you do if you no longer allowed fear to rule your life? Would you get on an airplane and travel to see different parts of the world? Would you start a business that would allow you to be home with your children? Would you call a friend or loved one that you have a strained relationship with to finally heal some past heart wounds? Would you finally go on that mission trip you have always dreamed about? Would you be open to God bringing you a spouse, even if you had been in a past relationship that was abusive, or if your past relationship left your heart badly broken? What would you do for God and for yourself if fear were no longer an issue in your life?

My sincere prayer is that you will be encouraged and know that God is always at work in your life. Even when a particular situation seems very scary, or a trial feels like there is no possible way for good to come out of it, He always has a plan. I want you to know for certain that *God is Good All the Time* and His plan is always best. You do not have to fear the future. I love what Max Lucado said in the following passage: "What you and I might rate as an absolute disaster, God may rate as a pimple-level problem that will pass. He views your life the way you view a movie after you've read the book. When something bad happens, you feel the air sucked out of the theatre. Everyone else gasps at the crisis on the screen. Not you. Why? You've read the book. You know how the good guy gets out of the tight spot. God views your life with the same confidence. He's not only read your story.... He wrote it."[21]

Friend, the hard reality is that the story of your life will eventually end. This is something you can count on. The most important question you need to answer is whether or not your eternal life is insured. I want you to know beyond a shadow of a doubt that you will spend eternity with your heavenly Father. There are no strategies or good deeds that will get you there. The only way to have eternal life is a relationship with Jesus Christ. If you ignore everything else in this book, please do not ignore the gospel of Jesus Christ and the eternal hope that is found in

Him alone. "For God so loved the world that he gave his one and only Son, that whoever believes in him shall not perish but have eternal life." (John 3:16 NIV)

I want to make myself very clear. The insurance question I am most concerned about is your eternal life. However, your children and dependents are also very important. One of the most loving things you can do for your family is to provide for them financially when you pass away. Life insurance is designed to protect family members from severe financial strain at the exact time that they are grieving from the loss of a family member. If you are financially responsible for any dependents, you need to protect their future if something unforeseen happens to you.

One common mistake I see couples make quite frequently is that they assume they do not need life insurance on a spouse that does not work outside of the home. Do not underestimate the value of the time and service this person provides for your family just because he or she does not collect a traditional paycheck. If you sat down to calculate how much it would cost to outsource the following services for your family, I think you would be quite shocked:

- Personal assistant to run errands and do laundry
- Culinary chef to grocery shop and prepare all meals
- Full time nanny to take care of the children when the other spouse is working full time
- A chauffer to carpool kids to and from activities

It would be quite expensive to pay all of the service providers you would need to replace your spouse who does not work outside of the home. Please do not forget to insure the spouse who helps keep your house running smoothly and most importunately, your children well taken care of. There are many types of life insurance that can be purchased. Life insurance provides either a lump sum of cash or an ongoing income stream for a policyholder's family if he or she suddenly dies. A life insurance policy can be used for many purposes, like:

- Replacement of income upon your death if you are still working
- Funeral expenses
- Pay off any outstanding medical bills
- Eliminate any other debts, such as credit cards, at your death
- Pay off your mortgage so your loved ones own a home free and clear of any debt
- Cover any potential estate tax liability at your death
- Save for a college education for your children or grandchildren
- Retirement planning

A life insurance policy has many business uses as well, including:

- Purchasing a surviving partners' interest in a business in the event of the death of a business partner. The terms of the deal are stated in a buy-sell agreement
- Deferred compensation arrangements for key employees that encourage retention
- Replace lost business income caused by the death of a key employee
- Funding qualified retirement plans like profit sharing plans and defined benefit plans

In order to make an informed decision before purchasing a new policy or contract, you need to understand what you are buying. Sadly, some insurance agents are only concerned with "selling" a product in order to make a commission. Always do your due diligence on the person from whom you are buying life insurance.

One example of a product available today is term life insurance. Typically, it is quite inexpensive. However, it may or may not be the best choice for your particular situation. This is why you always need to seek wise counsel. Let's talk about the different types of life insurance products available today and how to determine the amount of life insurance your family needs. One size does not fit all.

Term life insurance, or term assurance, is life insurance that provides coverage at a fixed rate of payments for a limited period of time, usually 10, 20 or a maximum of 30 years. After the term of the policy expires, coverage at the previous rate of premiums is no longer guaranteed. The policyholder must then decide whether or not they still need life insurance. At that time, they can either forgo coverage, or obtain new coverage with different payments or conditions. If the person who is insured dies during the term of the policy, the death benefit will be paid to his or her beneficiary. A little known fact about all life insurance policies is that the death benefit is paid to the beneficiaries of the policy tax-free. This is quite an attractive feature of life insurance.

Term life insurance policies can be contrasted to permanent life insurance policies like whole life, universal life, variable life, and variable universal life, which guarantee coverage at fixed premiums for the lifetime of the covered individual. Permanent insurance coverage stays in place for the life of the insured, even if they are in poor health. The insurance policies only lapse if the policy owner stops paying the premiums.

Preservation of money, and stable investment returns are two reasons that permanent insurance policies have become very popular. A portion of each premium paid goes into a cash-value account, or an investment account, depending on the type of policy. The funds inside of the life insurance policy grow on a tax-deferred basis. My clients have accessed cash inside permanent insurance policies to supplement college savings needs, pay for health care expenses or other emergencies, add to retirement savings, or invest in real estate. My clients like the fact that they are in control of how they use the cash inside of their insurance policy. Another benefit of permanent insurance is that the cash inside of the policy is protected from creditors in the event of a lawsuit. There are various types of permanent insurance policies and they all come with different durations, structures, costs, and variations.

Whole Life Insurance
This coverage offers guaranteed insurance for the duration of the policyholder's life. Such policies include a tax-deferred cash value that increases until the contract has been surrendered. Premiums for whole life insurance policies remain unchanged, and the policyholder has a guaranteed death benefit.

Universal Life Insurance
This insurance is much like whole life insurance, except that the protection, premiums and cash value can all be adjusted during the term of the contract. The cash values also accrue interest at a rate set by the insurance company.

Variable Life Insurance
These policies combine aspects of an investment fund with a whole life insurance policy.

Variable Universal Life Insurance
Variable universal life insurance (often shortened to VUL) is a type of life insurance that builds cash value inside of the policy.

My family has personally benefitted from having a Variable Universal Life Insurance Policy. My father purchased a VUL policy about 20 years ago with a lump sum of cash he received as an inheritance. The lump sum of cash he initially invested inside of the contract was sufficient to pay the premiums for the life insurance in perpetuity and still have cash inside of the policy. He did have his insurance agent monitor the cash value inside of his policy every year to make sure he did not need to contribute any more funds to cover the annual premiums. Over time, he was able to invest and grow the cash value portion inside of the policy.

My father is now 75 years old and retired. The life insurance provides a lump sum of cash for his beneficiaries at his death. In addition, he can take loans from the cash value of the insurance while he is alive and pay for large ticket items he needs during retirement that are not part of his monthly budget. He was able to buy a new 2013 Ford Explorer with some of the accumulated cash value inside of the policy two years ago. He took the funds as a loan but it did not impact the premium payments. It was quite important that he was able to get the new car at Age 73 since the car he replaced was ten years old. He also had the joy of giving the former car to his grandson when he turned 16 and got his driver's license. The car will be a great help to his family in helping car pool five brothers and sisters to and from school and various extra-curricular activities. It is rewarding for me to see how financial planning with life insurance has made a positive impact on multiple generations of my extended family.

One of the questions I am often asked is, "How much life insurance do I need to protect my family?" There is a way to calculate how much life insurance you really need to safely cover the financial needs of your dependents. This is a nugget I am sharing in this book for free. I often use this spreadsheet with my clients in my financial planning practice. My sincere desire is that you can utilize this tool to make a wise decision regarding the purchase of life insurance for your family. Trust me, you do not want to be under-insured, or pay too much in premiums and be over- insured.

How Much Life Insurance Do You Need To Protect Your Family?

Income:

1. Total annual income your family would need if you died today: $_____
What your family needs, before taxes, to maintain its current standard of living (Typically between 60% - 75% of total income)

2. Annual income your family would receive from other sources: $_____
Dividends, interest income, spouse's earnings (Social Security may be available)

3. Income to be replaced: Subtract line 2 from line 1: $_____

4. Capital needed for income: $_____
Multiply line 3 by appropriate factor in Table A:

Expenses:

5. Funeral and other final expenses: $_____
The average cost of an adult funeral is about $6,130

6. Mortgage and other outstanding debts: $_____
Include mortgage balance, credit card debt, car loans, etc.

7. College costs for each child, in today's dollars: $_____

Average 4-year costs; state college or university = $60,000 (in-state resident), private college or out of state university = $100,000+

8. Capital needed for college: $_____
Multiply line 7 by the appropriate factor in Table B

9. Total capital required: $_____
Add lines 4, 5, 6 and 8

Assets:

10. Savings and investments: $_____
Bank accounts, money market accounts, CDs, stocks, bonds, mutual funds, etc.

11. Retirement savings: $_____
IRAs, 401(k)s, Keoghs, pension and profit sharing plans

12. Present amount of life insurance: $_____
Include group insurance as well as insurance purchased on your own

13. Total income producing assets: $_____
Add lines 10, 11 and 12

14. Life insurance needed: $_____
Subtract line 13 from line 9

TABLE A

Years	Income needed Factor
10	8.1
15	11.1
20	13.6
25	15.6
30	17.3
35	18.7
40	20.0

TABLE B

Years Before college	Factor
5	.82
10	.68
15	.56
20	.46

Important note: Inflation is assumed to be 4%. The rate of return on investments is assumed to be 8%. Changing either or both of these assumptions would change the results. Life insurance is an important part of your overall financial plan. Do not underestimate its value. It can help provide financial security if you unexpectedly pass away when you still have family members who are dependent upon you to help provide for their needs. It is a gift to provide financial security to your loved ones, whether you are alive or not. Consider taking action today to determine if you have enough insurance or you need to apply for more coverage. Don't delay! The future is not certain.

11

If You Ever Become Disabled, How Will You Pay Your Bills?

Not only so, but we also glory in our sufferings, because we know that suffering produces perseverance; perseverance, character; and character, hope. And hope does not put us to shame, because God's love has been poured out into our hearts through the Holy Spirit, who has been given to us.

Romans 5:3-5 NIV

I recently had the privilege of getting to know a new friend named Trent. Honestly, his story is quite tragic. However, he has inspired me to count my blessings and remain faithful. Trent has learned that he had no choice but to fully rely on God for his daily needs. I now believe that his dependency on God for his daily provision is a healthier attitude than falsely believing that we are in control, and the weight of the world is on our shoulders.

Trent and his family would have been completely devastated financially if he had not purchased long term disability insurance before becoming paralyzed as a result of a rare auto-immune disorder. Trent's testimony is told best in his own words.

> *Emily,*
> *Thank you for the opportunity to tell my story. I hope it encourages your readers to purchase long term disability insurance. It's a very small price to pay to protect your*

family from being poverty stricken, after an unforeseen illness or injury.

After we got married, my wife and I lived in West Palm, Florida for about 10 years. I worked in a management position and my wife worked as a teacher. From the beginning of my career, I always purchased the Cadillac of insurance plans for my health coverage. This also included any supplemental benefits that my company offered.

My employer offered short-term disability insurance paid by the company. Most importantly, I also had the option to purchase long-term disability insurance. Believe it or not, the after tax cost of my long-term disability insurance was only $1.61 per month. The insurance guaranteed 60% of my income if I ever became permanently disabled. Since I paid my portion of the required insurance premiums after tax, the benefits could not be taxed twice. As a result, my benefits would be tax free should I ever need them.

Honestly, I never thought I would need to use my short-term or long-term disability insurance benefits. However, since the cost of the monthly premiums was less than the average cost of a cup of coffee, I decided it was a wise financial move to apply for disability coverage.

We always planned for my wife, Nicole, to work as a teacher until we had children. Then she would be a stay at home mom and homeschool our children. However, God had a different plan. Nicole became pregnant with twins in 2010. Unfortunately, she experienced a very difficult pregnancy and our twins were born prematurely in May of 2011. As a result, both of our babies had a lot of medical complications. Some of the medical expenses necessary to keep them alive in the NICU were not completely covered by our health insurance. We quickly drained our savings to pay for our children's healthcare needs. Eventually, our twins were healthy enough to leave the hospital and come home in July of 2011. We were so grateful that our babies were alive and healthy. We were looking forward to getting back on our feet financially and starting our lives as a family of four. Believe it or not, I broke my ankle the day after we brought the twins home from the hospital for the first time. I had to have surgery and be on short-term disability until I recovered.

On December 16, 2011, I unexpectedly became paralyzed by a very rare autoimmune condition called Guillain-Barre Syndrome. It came on very fast. Due to an error in the paperwork from the ER to the ICU, I was not treated with the correct medicine that could have given me back full mobility. Since I had taken so much time off of work when our twins were in the NICU, I had no more paid vacation. I had also used up my short term disability benefits when I broke my ankle. I immediately went onto long-term disability. I spent a month and a half in a hospital rehabilitation treatment center. Thank goodness I had disability insurance to provide income for our family.

After seeing some improvement in my condition and moving back to Texas in April of 2012, I started to decline again. Specialists then diagnosed me with a progressive form of CIDP (Chronic Inflammatory Demyelinating Polyneuropathy). Our healthcare costs continued to grow. I needed constant physical therapy as well as ongoing medical treatments. Nicole went back to work as a teacher and our twins were put into daycare.

However, God did not forget us or forsake us. He answered our prayers for funds to sustain our family. My employer found a small pension that I didn't even know existed. The pension gave us a small amount of money that allowed us to rent a home, and move forward. We continued to pray and reach out to those who would pray with us, and provide emotional support and friendship. We were blessed again when our friends raised money to help sustain us financially. We even received money to purchase a wheelchair lift to accommodate a van so that I could drive.

I believe that we are all naturally people who dream about tomorrow. We want to work and provide for our families, and then eventually retire. However, our paradigm has completely shifted. We now have new dreams; ones that have adapted to our new normal and with God as our leader. God was with me when I decided to pay that small $1.61 premium for disability insurance. Without that decision, we would have no home and be dependent on social services. Instead, we have a roof over our head, a car to get to church, and my wife has a job. As I am writing this letter, we are sitting on the sofa with our beautiful, four-year old twins.
God is good,
Trent.[22]

Friend, please consider purchasing long-term disability insurance, either through your employer, or an individual policy. Group benefit policies are usually less expensive if you have access to disability coverage through your employer. However, if you leave your current job, your insurance may not be portable to take with you. You can purchase an individual disability policy from an insurance agent. It may be slightly more expensive than group coverage, but you own the policy as long as you continue to pay the premiums. It does not matter if you change jobs, as long as you are in the same occupation.

Did you know that you are much more likely to become disabled than die? According to the U.S. Census Bureau, nearly 1 in 5 people have a disability in the United States[23]. If you are not able to work because of health issues, you should have a backup plan to cover your monthly fixed expenses, as well as your medical care. I want to encourage you to stop and ask yourself the following question: "If I get sick or injured and can no longer work, will I be able to pay my bills and maintain my current standard of living?" If the answer to this question is no, please don't get discouraged. There are practical ways to plan for a disability from a financial standpoint. Let's start with a simple quiz to see how much you know about personal disability insurance.

If You Ever Become Disabled,
How Will You Pay Your Bills

Quiz: How Much Do You Know About Disability Insurance?

You probably don't hesitate to insure assets such as your house and automobile, but you may not have coverage for another valuable asset: your ability to generate income. When consumers were asked questions about disability insurance in a LIMRA survey, only 4% demonstrated a high level of knowledge. This short quiz may help gauge your understanding of "paycheck insurance."[24]

1. What are the odds that an American entering the workforce today will become disabled before retiring?

    a. 1 in 10

    b. 1 in 5

    c. 1 in 3

2. Disabilities are usually caused by catastrophic events such as serious accidents or injuries.

    a. True

    b. False

3. What percentage of American workers has disability income insurance?

    a. 67%

    b. 44%

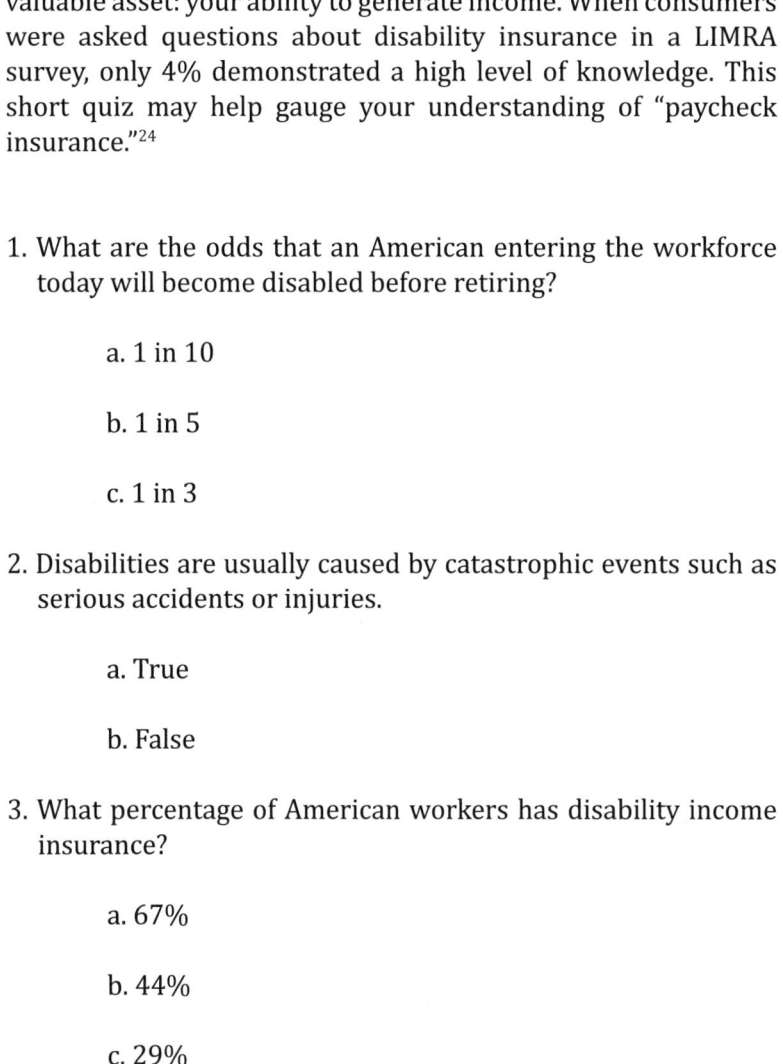

    c. 29%

Answers to Quiz:

1. c. 1 in 3

2. b. False. Only 9% of disabilities result from serious accidents. Top causes include common illnesses and chronic medical conditions such as back pain and arthritis.

3. c. 29%[25]

Here's the most important thing you should know: A disability income insurance policy could replace a percentage of your income (up to the policy limits) if you are unable to work as a result of an injury or illness. Benefits may be paid for a specified number of years, or until you reach retirement age. Some policies may pay benefits if you cannot work in your current occupation; others may pay only if you cannot work in any type of job.

You could become disabled after an accident, injury, or as a result of an illness. If you or a loved one ever becomes disabled, please remember that God can use affliction and physical disabilities for our good, even though the process may be extremely painful. Remember what the Apostle Paul wrote about his own affliction: "Therefore, in order to keep me from becoming conceited, I was given a thorn in my flesh, a messenger of Satan, to torment me. Three times I pleaded with the Lord to take it away from me. But he said to me, "My grace is sufficient for you, for my power is made perfect in weakness." Therefore I will boast all the more gladly about my weaknesses, so that Christ's power may rest on me. That is why, for Christ's sake, I delight in weaknesses, in insults, in hardships, in persecutions, in difficulties. For when I am weak, then I am strong." (2 Corinthians 12:7-10 NIV)

In my experience, I have never met anyone who thought they were going to have a car accident, become paralyzed, or find out that they have cancer before the day it happened. When the accident occurred, or the doctor called with the diagnosis, everything in their life changed in an instant. Time stood still. Questions came at lightning speed. What does this mean for me?

If You Ever Become Disabled, How Will You Pay Your Bills

Will I live? If I do live, will I be miserable physically? Who will pay for my health care needs if I cannot work? Who will take care of my kids? I don't want to be a burden to my family. How am I going to survive?

I recommend carrying enough personal disability insurance to replace at least 60 percent of your earnings, if you ever become disabled. Your ability to generate income is one of your most valuable resources. Please do not forget to insure it. Many insurance companies limit disability benefits to between 50 percent and 80 percent from all sources of disability income, prior to the disability. For example, if you also qualify for Social Security disability benefits, those payments you receive could be deducted from your benefit amount from your own insurance policy. Some individual policies will pay you partial benefits if you can only work part-time as a result of sickness or an injury. Individual policies specify how much you will be paid, how soon after you are disabled that benefits will begin, and when benefits will end.

If you do become disabled and are covered by insurance, the monthly benefits will be payable for a fixed period of time. Your specific benefits will always be outlined in your policy contract. The most common benefit periods for disability insurance are: 2 years, 5 years, to age 65, or for the rest of your life, while disability continues. The longer your insurance will pay you benefits, the higher the premiums will cost. One strategy for reducing the cost of a disability insurance policy is to extend the waiting period, which is the time between when the disability occurs and when you start receiving benefits. Choosing a 90-day or 180-day waiting period (instead of 30 days) may help lower your premium cost. There are two additional features of disability income policies that I want you to understand. The terms can be confusing.

- Non-cancelable protection means that your insurance policy's premium can never be raised above the amount shown in the policy, and benefits may not be reduced, as long as the premiums for the policy are paid on time.
- Guaranteed renewable is a feature that gives the owner

of the policy the right to renew his or her policy, with the same benefits, but the insurer can increase your premiums. The insurance company can only raise premiums for coverage if they are increasing the premiums for all other policyholders in the same class (i.e., having the same characteristics).

There are also many riders, or optional benefits, that you can now purchase when buying personal disability insurance. I want you to be an informed consumer so I have outlined the most common disability insurance riders available today:

Future Purchase Option (Guaranteed Insurability Option)

This rider allows the insured to buy more disability income insurance if his or her income increases, without providing proof of medical insurability. In other words, the owner of the policy never has to have a medical exam or physical again. Even if you develop a medical condition that would normally prevent you from obtaining additional coverage after you purchase your original policy, you could still increase your benefits if you have proof that your income has increased.

Cost of Living Adjustments (COLA)

This rider provides an annual increase in benefits. The percentage of increase is usually based on a Consumer Price Index, or a predetermined percentage, such as 3% or 5% annually. This is a very important feature. A COLA allows your benefits to increase annually in order to keep pace with inflation.

Residual Benefit

This rider pays the insured a portion of the monthly disability benefit if he or she has a reduction in income due to a disability. In most cases, this happens when the owner of the policy has gone back to work but is only able to work part time. Ordinarily, the insured must satisfy a minimum percentage loss in earnings to qualify.

Social Security Rider

This rider pays you a benefit even if you are not able to receive Social Security disability benefits because of the Social Security Administration's definition of disability.

Please remember that all types of insurance are designed to protect the owner of the policy from the worst-case scenario. My sincere hope is that you will never need to use disability income insurance in your lifetime. That is the best-case scenario. However, as we all know, there are no guarantees in life. That is why insurance was invented. It protects you and your family from financial ruin if you become, sick, injured, or die while you still have financial responsibilities to support your loved ones.

The premiums for long-term disability insurance are worth the peace of mind that it will give you and your family. You will be able to rest in the knowledge that if something unforeseen happens to you medically during your prime working years, you won't also be devastated financially. If you are still questioning whether or not this is a good investment, let me remind you that it is not an investment. It is insurance. That is why you should consult a knowledgeable professional that can assist you in purchasing the best possible insurance for the lowest possible premium dollars. In summary, don't forget to consider disability insurance as part of your overall financial plan.

12

Growing Older is Easier With Some Extra Help

Stand up in the presence of the aged, show respect for the elderly and revere your God. I am the Lord.

Leviticus: 19:32 NIV

I am personally in the life stage called *the sandwich*. That means that I have both aging parents and young children at the same time. My parents are now in there 70s, and I am now F-O-R-T-Y years old. It honestly is very difficult for me to believe. I have no idea how it happened. Then I glance at a mirror and I realize I need to pluck a grey hair out of the crown of my head. If the sun is shining just right, I can clearly see all of my newly acquired "sparkles".

My children are still young because I did not have my first child until I was almost 32 years old. I am the mother of a nine year-old daughter and a five year-old son. My plate is rather full. If you find yourself in the sandwich stage of life, it can be quite a challenge, both financially and emotionally, if you and your family are not properly prepared.

In the year 2000, I worked as a private banker for JP Morgan Chase Private Bank in Dallas. I provided financial planning and investment management advice to high net worth individuals. I quickly learned the importance of long-term care insurance for aging individuals and couples. If a person becomes very ill and/

or disabled, they could potentially require home health care and assistance with the daily acts of living, or full time care in a nursing home. The purpose of long-term care insurance is to pay for the costs of this type of medical care, which can be very expensive. A nursing home currently costs around $5,000 to $6,000 per month. If a person is not independently wealthy, or what we refer to as self-insured, then these expenses can completely erode an individual's or a couple's savings and investments set-aside for retirement.

The solution from a financial planning perspective is to purchase long-term care insurance for your loved ones before they reach the age and stage of life when they need extensive medical care. Otherwise, the family will have to pay cash for the expenses related to home health care, or a nursing home. Unexpected medical expenses are the number one risk factor for eroding a family's retirement savings. If you become completely indigent, meaning you have exhausted all of your financial resources, you could qualify for Medicaid. However, a nursing home paid for by Medicaid will be far from ideal care for you, or your loved ones.

Many people mistakenly think that once they turn 65, and are eligible for Medicare, that the insurance will also cover any long-term care needs in a nursing home if ever necessary. *This is false information.* Medicare *only* covers medically necessary acute care, such as doctor's visits, drugs, and hospital stays. Medicare coverage also focuses on short-term services for conditions that are expected to improve, such as physical therapy to help you regain your function after a fall or stroke.

I personally encouraged my parents to purchase long-term care insurance while they were still young and healthy so that the premiums for the insurance would be affordable. The two major factors for determining how expensive the premiums will be for a long-term care insurance policy are a person's age and current health status. Please remember that insurance never gets cheaper if you wait a year to buy it in order to save money. Unfortunately, you cannot help but get older every year, even if you are still in good health. Furthermore, an individual can be completely denied coverage if an insurance company believes they are too risky to insure. I personally have several clients that were denied coverage because they waited too long to apply for this type of insurance.

In 2001, my parents went to a holiday party between Christmas and New Year's Day, an ordinary function for that time of the year. We had no warning signs that my father's life was about to change. During the dinner party, he gradually became extremely dizzy and nauseated after eating a normal meal with some close friends they had known for years.

Fortunately, one of the guests at the party was in the medical field and knew immediately that my father's symptoms were not related to a stomach virus or food sensitivity: he was on the verge of having a heart attack. My father thought his friend was overreacting, but reluctantly allowed his friend to rush him to the nearest emergency room. His doctors immediately confirmed that he was in critical condition and he did in fact need immediate medical attention.

When my brother and I heard the news, we both drove as fast as possible to the hospital. I remember parking my car and running inside to find my parents in the Cardiac ICU. I was in such shock that I had no idea where I parked my car when I finally went to find it again. I am telling you this story so you will know that I speak from experience that life can change in the blink of an eye. The point of the story is not to scare you. It is actually to teach you how to proactively plan for this type of situation from a financial planning perspective.

The physician said my father needed triple bypass heart surgery. He was definitely not leaving the hospital any time soon. He ended up having heart bypass surgery on New Year's Eve. This was the first time in my life that I experienced the true reality that I might lose my father, something very frightening. Fortunately, my father's surgery was a success, and God still had many plans for his life. My father eventually recovered from his heart surgery, but it was a very long journey. We were incredibly grateful that he was still alive and with our family. However, his cardiologist told us that it was not a matter of if, but when, he would have another heart issue. That is difficult news to live with from a patient's point of view, as well as for the family members who love and depend on the person who has health challenges.

Before my father got sick, our family purchased a joint long-term care insurance policy that would provide benefits for both of my parents if either one ever needed extensive medical care. I honestly hoped that they would never have to use the insurance. I knew from a risk mitigation standpoint that it was more prudent and cost effective to purchase a joint policy that both of my parents could benefit from financially, rather than an individual policy that would only provide benefits if one person became very ill. I had counseled many people already by that stage of my career. I was well aware that no one knows what the future holds. I always tell my clients, "It is best to plan for the worst case scenario, and hope for the best case scenario."

Fortunately, with the help of modern medicine, my father's heart condition and blood pressure continue to be well controlled. He just celebrated his 75th birthday, and he is still actively working in his ministry fourteen years after his heart surgery. He is not the type of retiree who plays golf or goes fishing a lot. He is passionate about using the time he has here on earth to further God's kingdom and bring more people to Christ. He actually is the only private citizen in history to build more than one chapel in Texas state prisons. His ministry, Chapel of Hope Ministries, Inc. completed its first prison chapel in 1997 at Hutchins State Jail in Dallas. Seven more chapels followed. Inmates and ministry volunteers flooded in. Today, these eight chapels alone host an estimated 80,000 inmate visits and 15,000 volunteer visits every year.

My mother has also been an active part of my father's ministry. However, about five years ago we started noticing that my mother's short-term memory was declining. She was still very active physically, but she was starting to show signs of confusion when it came to analyzing certain situations, and her short-term memory seemed to be declining rapidly. She was also struggling with chronic back pain and depression.

My father and I spent a great amount of time at various

specialists with my mother to determine what the underlying cause of her health issues was. In the beginning, physicians told us that her health issues were related to declining hormones during menopause. That theory eventually proved to be wrong, so we began to think that her memory issues and depression were related to dealing with chronic back pain.

Another specialist told us that she was clinically depressed, which was supposedly the root cause of her issues with short-term memory and chronic back pain. It really was a case of which came first: the chicken or the egg? Each time we were given a new explanation for her health challenges, we were optimistic that the new plan for her medical care would allow her to make a full recovery. However, so far, God has had other plans for my mother. We now know that my mother is actually suffering from dementia. Remember, we all have challenges. They just look differently for each person. I will never understand why this has happened this side of heaven, but I now know that I cannot fix the problem. My only job is to love my mother well in her current state of health. My job is not to question the goodness or faithfulness of God. Interestingly, if you ask my mother, she would tell you that she is the most blessed woman on earth. She has two grown children who love and adore her, and eight healthy, active grandchildren. She is the picture of grace during a difficult trial. She loves God with all of her heart, mind, and soul.

After my father had triple bypass heart surgery, I always thought that he would be the one to need part time care, or full-time care in a nursing home, sometime in the future. For the majority of the time that my parents have had their long term care insurance in place, it was never on my radar that my mom would be the one to benefit from the insurance.

After my mother received a formal diagnosis of dementia in 2013, she was able to begin collecting financial benefits from my parents' joint long-term care insurance. The financial benefits from her insurance have made all of the difference in the world in terms of both of my parents' quality of life. One of the benefits of being medically qualified for financial benefits from your insurance is that you can stop paying the monthly or annual premiums. My father got a raise during retirement when he no longer had to cover the monthly insurance premiums with his fixed income.

In my mother's case, we want her to stay in her own home as long as possible, and God-willing, indefinitely. The good news from a financial planning standpoint is that my parents' long-term care insurance covers the salary of a sweet caregiver for my mother. She comes to their home each day to help my mom with cooking, organizing the house, cleaning, and driving. She also is a good companion for my mother, so she still has daily social contact with someone besides just my father. Many patients with dementia tend to become anti-social, so it is very important to keep them socialized. In addition, my father can still travel for meetings and events related to his prison ministry. Otherwise, he would be unable to leave my mother at home alone to continue the work God has called him to do.

The reality of life is that we do not know what the future holds. Thank God we can rest in the fact that God does have a plan for each and every one of us. I am grateful that God has given me the tools to help people just like you to mitigate the financial burdens that can arise unexpectedly in life. I can assure you that God does provide for each and every one of us, and He is Faithful.

If you or a loved one is in their fifties or sixties, it would be prudent to investigate the cost of purchasing long term care insurance. It does not cost anything to apply for coverage. You should contact a reputable insurance sales person, who is experienced with helping clients navigate the underwriting process for long term care insurance.

There are many variables to consider when purchasing long-term care insurance:

1. You must choose a waiting period before insurance benefits begin. The average waiting period is 90 to 180 days. The longer the waiting period, the cheaper the premiums for the insurance will cost. However, if you do not have enough money to cover the medical care during the waiting period, then you need to select a shorter

waiting period.

2. You also need to select a monthly benefit amount. I usually recommend at least $5,000 per month.

3. I advise my clients to select a cost of living adjustment (COLA) benefit so their insurance benefits keep up with inflation. The average COLA is 3 to 5% per year.

4. When applying for coverage, you also need to select a time period for how long the benefits will last. Typically, you can continue to receive coverage for medical expenses in a nursing home for three to five years. However, if you end up utilizing home health care rather than care in a nursing home, your pool of money from your insurance will last longer.

5. Make sure that you purchase coverage that offers flexibility for how you utilize your benefits if you, or your spouse, ever need them.

As you can see, purchasing long term care insurance is *not* something you want to purchase online, or from an agent who is not experienced. Always seek wise counsel from a licensed insurance agent or financial advisor, whom you know, or who has been referred to you by a trusted resource. Also, consider taking time to educate yourself on the different options you may want to add to a policy for yourself, your spouse, or your parents. If you are an educated consumer, you will have more realistic information about the types of policies, options for coverage, premiums, and riders available in the market place today.

13

When Can I Transition From Making Money to Spending It?

Whatever you do, work at it with all your heart, as working for the Lord, not for human masters, since you know that you will receive an inheritance from the Lord as a reward. It is the Lord Christ you are serving.

Colossians 3:23-24 NIV

One of my favorite illustrations of a successful transition from working full time to enjoying her retirement years is my friend, Mrs. Goldman. She and her husband were both educators, working hard for over 30 years both as teachers and school administrators. They were quite frugal and always made sure to fully participate in their teacher retirement plans. They were never wealthy by the world's standards, but they lived a comfortable middle class lifestyle throughout their adult lives on the East Coast. They were the proud parents of twin boys that they made sure were educated well and successfully launched into careers of their own.

Unfortunately, Mr. Goldman died in 2007 unexpectedly, just before he and Mrs. Goldman were officially going to retire from the school districts where they had worked for so many years.

Mr. Goldman never got to enjoy his retirement with Mrs. Goldman. However, he did give Mrs. Goldman the gift of being financially prepared for his passing. He left a legacy of loving

God, working hard, and making wise financial decisions for his wife and his sons. Mr. Goldman had a generous life insurance policy that provided for his wife and their twin boys, as well as a will and an estate plan that were both very well thought out. He was also extremely organized, an amazing gift to leave for the beneficiaries of your estate.

His careful financial planning allowed Mrs. Goldman time to grieve before making any long-term decisions about how she would live in retirement as a single widow, rather than with her husband as she always envisioned. This was a shattered dream for Mrs. Goldman. However, after taking time to grieve, pray, consult her friends and family, she decided to move to Texas to spend her retirement years close to one of her sons and her beloved grandchildren.

This is when I met Mrs. Goldman for the very first time. We immediately had a lot in common. She is very wise, but also quite funny, even though I do not think she intends to be. Every time I gave her advice she would proclaim, "from your mouth to God's ears." My husband and I use that phrase often now in our own lives. One of the first things she did from a financial planning perspective was to create a realistic monthly budget. Together, we reviewed her monthly recurring expenses and then decided how much she could afford to spend each month in retirement. She had a pension from the school district, but she needed to supplement her monthly income. She used a portion of her assets to buy an annuity. An annuity will provide her with additional income each month. She purchased her annuity inside an IRA so she is only taxed as she takes income out of the annuity over time, and not all at once. The annuity provided her with the following benefits:

- A guaranteed income stream for life that she could never outlive
- Access to cash inside of the annuities if she ever has a liquidity need
- A death benefit for her two sons

When Can I Transition From Making Money to Spending It?

It was very important to Mrs. Goldman to leave assets to her sons and grandsons as part of her legacy. Therefore, she decided to use some of her taxable assets to pay for a term life insurance policy with a lump sum of cash to replace some of her investments she would use to live on while alive. She also used a portion of her taxable trust funds to pay off the small mortgage she had on her new home in Texas. That allowed Mrs. Goldman to live debt free as well as rent-free. The remaining trust funds were invested in a conservative investment portfolio that she could access if needed. She uses some of these funds each year to travel the world with her dear friends from the synagogue.

As we fast forward to 2015, Mrs. Goldman is the poster child for a successful transition into retirement, even though her journey has not been easy. I have seen her blossom and become a very strong, independent and inspiring woman. She is very involved in the lives of her grandchildren, and she hosts all of the Jewish holidays at her home with her family. She is also a docent at our local modern art museum. The museum has inspired her so much artistically that she now also takes classes to learn how to paint with watercolors. She travels all over the world, literally, as she says, "while I still can." She is busier in retirement than she was when she was working full time.

Most people spend a large portion of their adult life accumulating assets. We work so that we can have money to cover our family's needs. If we are wise, we save a portion of our income every month. How do we know when we can finally stop working and start living off of the income that our assets will provide?

This transition period is called "moving from the accumulation phase of assets to the annuitization of assets." It may sound like fancy, financial jargon, but it is a very important aspect of financial planning. Accumulation of assets simply means working and saving money. Annuitization of assets means taking the money you already have, and figuring out how to create an income stream for yourself.

The decline of traditional pensions, combined with longer life spans and rising medical expenses, has created an uncertain future for many Americans, including those who have put away a solid nest egg for retirement. Many people are fearful that they are going to out-live their retirement savings. This is one of the reasons you should consider purchasing an annuity.

An annuity is a contract between you and insurance company, in which you make a lump sum payment or series of payments, and in return, you receive regular disbursements beginning either immediately or at some point in the future. The goal of annuities is to provide a steady stream of income during retirement.

There are a lot of different types of annuities in the market place today. They offer various features and benefits that you can choose to fit your particular situation. For example, you can now lock in downside protection and still benefit from upside growth in the stock market. You can also lock in favorable interest rates. I strongly suggest that you set up a consultation with a professional financial advisor to help guide you during this important life stage. Please make sure the advisor you work with has experience working with retirees specifically.

Below is a list of the most common reasons that individuals and couples preparing for retirement consider purchasing annuities:

- Deferral of taxes is a big benefit.
- The ability to put large sums of money into an annuity, more than is allowed annually in a 401(k) plan or an IRA, all at once or over a period of time.
- Flexible payout options that can help retirees meet their cash-flow needs.
- Offers a death benefit; generally, if the contract owner or annuitant dies before the annuitization stage, the beneficiary will receive a death benefit at least equal to the net premiums paid.
- Annuities can help an estate avoid probate; beneficiaries receive the annuity proceeds without time delays and probate expenses.
- One of the most appealing benefits of an annuity is the option for a guaranteed lifetime income stream.

When Can I Transition From Making Money to Spending It?

- When you purchase an annuity contract, your annuity assets will accumulate tax deferred until you start taking withdrawals in retirement. Distributions of earnings are taxed as ordinary income. Withdrawals taken prior to age 59½ may be subject to a 10% federal income tax penalty.

Fixed annuities are annuity contracts with insurance companies that pay a fixed rate of return. If you start receiving income immediately, the annuity is called an *immediate fixed annuity*. You can also purchase a fixed annuity, but postpone the income payments until a future date. This type of fixed annuity is called a *deferred fixed annuity*. Although the rate on a fixed annuity may be adjusted, it will never fall below a guaranteed minimum rate specified in the annuity contract. This guaranteed rate acts as a floor to help protect owners from periods of low interest rates.

Variable annuities offer fluctuating investment returns. The owner of a variable annuity allocates premiums among his or her choice to investment sub-accounts. When a variable annuity is surrendered, or "cashed in", the value of the annuity may be worth more or less than the original amount invested.

Variable annuities have been a bit controversial over the years. They are more complex products than simple, fixed annuities. There are different pros and cons to consider. Like medicine, variable annuities can be very beneficial for some retirees, but disastrous for others. I suggest educating yourself on the pros and cons of variable annuities so you can decide whether or not a variable annuity makes sense for your unique financial plan. Variable annuity subaccounts are designed to imitate mutual funds; which allow investors to invest their money to grow and receive high rates of return.

Whether or not you decide to purchase an annuity as part of your retirement plan, please be aware of a common mistake I often see individuals and couples make. They mistakenly choose to allocate all of their discretionary income toward college savings needs for children and then *not* save for retirement. For example, a family has kids in high school with plans to go off to college in just a few short years. Retirement, on the other hand, seems very far away for the parents. In reality, college students can get financial aid. They can also work while going to school and help pay for some of their own expenses if necessary. However, parents cannot take out a loan for retirement. Please do not misunderstand me. I am *not* advocating that you not save for a college education for your child. I want to clarify that retirement savings has to be your first priority.

Another very important aspect of preparing for retirement involves how to best take out distributions from employer sponsored retirement plans, such as a 401k, upon retirement. Retirees are faced with a few broad options. Is it better to take the payout in the form of systematic payments, a lifetime annuity, or a lump sum? Let's discuss each strategy:

Systematic Withdrawals

Some retirement plans may allow you to take systematic withdrawals: either a fixed dollar amount on a regular schedule, a specific percentage of the account value on a regular schedule, or the total value of the account in equal distributions over a specified period of time.

The Lifetime Annuity Option

Your retirement plan may allow you to take payouts as a lifetime annuity, which converts your account balance into guaranteed monthly payments based on your life expectancy. If you live longer than expected, the payments continue anyway.

There are several advantages associated with this payout method. It helps you avoid the temptation to spend a significant amount of your assets at one time and the pressure to invest a large sum of money that might not last for the rest of your life. Also, there is no large initial tax bill on your entire nest egg; each monthly payment is taxed incrementally as ordinary income.

If you are married, you may have the option to elect a joint and survivor annuity. This would result in a lower monthly retirement payment than the single annuity option, but your spouse would continue to receive a portion of your retirement income after your death. If you do not elect an annuity with a survivor option, your monthly payments end with your death.

The main disadvantage of the annuity option lies in the potential reduction of spending power over time. Annuity payments are not indexed for inflation. If we experienced a 4% annual inflation rate, the purchasing power of the fixed monthly payment would be halved in 18 years.

Lump-Sum Distribution

If you elect to take the money from your employer-sponsored retirement plan as a single lump sum, you would receive the entire vested account balance in one payment, which you can invest and use as you see fit. You would retain control of the principal and could use it whenever and however you wish.

Of course, if you choose a lump sum, you will have to pay ordinary income taxes on the total amount of the distribution in one year. A large distribution could easily move you into a higher tax bracket. Another consideration is the 20% withholding rule: Employers issuing a check for a lump-sum distribution are required to withhold 20% toward federal income taxes. Thus, you would receive only 80% of your account balance, not 100%. Distributions taken prior to age 59½ are also subject to a 10% federal income tax penalty.

To avoid some of these tax issues, you can choose to roll the balance of the funds directly to an IRA in order to maintain the tax-deferred status of the funds. An IRA rollover might provide you with more options, not only in how you choose to invest the funds but also in how you access the funds over time.

Friend, I want you to understand that it really is possible to successfully transition from making money to spending money while in retirement, just like Mrs. Goldman at the top of this chapter. Here are some lessons from her life.

- Have a realistic monthly budget established at the beginning of your retirement. I suggest using the budget worksheet I included at the end of Chapter 2. Modify the budget to include only income you will have during retirement. In addition, determine which expenses will decrease or be eliminated after you retire from working (i.e. dry cleaning, gas, dining out, etc.) Your budget will most likely look a lot different during your retirement years.

- Your goal should be to have no debt and own a home free and clear before you stop working and retire. Owning your own home without a mortgage significantly increases your financial security. It also decreases your cost of living during retirement. If you have a large home with a mortgage, you should definitely consider selling your large home and paying cash for a much less expensive home. Smaller homes are also easier to maintain both physically and financially.
- Determine if there is a gap between the income you will receive automatically from pensions and/or social security, and what you will need each month to cover your monthly expenses.
- If there is an additional monthly income need, consider purchasing an annuity that will provide another income stream for you during retirement.
- Make sure you have a conservative investment portfolio for the remainder of your liquid assets that can provide you with upside growth potential, but significant downside protection. You will want the majority of your investment portfolio allocated to bonds, rather than stocks.
- Meet with a financial advisor to determine if you have enough assets to be self-insured, or if your estate could benefit from life insurance.
- If you retire prior to age 65, you will need health insurance. You cannot enroll in Medicare until age 65. Have a plan for how you will pay for your health insurance *before* you retire. A lot of people continue to work, at least part time, until Age 65 in order to keep their health insurance through their employer.

- You should also budget for Long Term Care insurance premiums unless your assets are significant enough that you are self-insured.
- Make sure your will and estate plan are current and match your desires for your estate and your beneficiaries.
- Consider creating a binder that contains all of your important financial documents in one place. Then store the binder in a very secure place such as a safety deposit box or a safe. This will allow the Executor of your estate to properly manage your affairs if something happens to you unexpectedly.

I hope you are inspired to evaluate your current financial situation. It takes a lot of pressure off of you not to have to worry about it if you have a plan in place. Please remember, focus on planning for living and not dying!

14

Proper Estate Planning is a Great Legacy

Whatever you do, work at it with all your heart, as working for the Lord, not for human masters, since you know that you will receive an inheritance from the Lord as a reward. It is the Lord Christ you are serving.

Colossians 3:23-24 (NIV)

My friend Elizabeth has experienced the death of two close family members in the last year. It has been a tough time of grieving and change for her and her family.

She learned first-hand during her grieving process what an incredible gift it is to the survivors, if the deceased family member had a well-thought-out estate plan, and a current will. Elizabeth's sister is now a widow with two young children. She has been able to take time to grieve because her husband had plenty of life insurance to support her and her small children. As a result, she was not forced to go back to work immediately upon her husband's death. She was a stay-at-home mom before her husband died. Since she received adequate life insurance proceeds, she has continued to be a stay at home mom. The life insurance proceeds have allowed her to create as much of a sense of normalcy as possible for her children while they were grieving as well.

Please don't misunderstand. Money never replaces a loved

one. However, if someone is going to die and leave a widow behind, it is a much better situation if she is not also financially devastated at the exact time that she is grieving and figuring out how to move on with her life.

Sadly, Elizabeth's mother-in-law *also* passed away recently. She was in her 80s and had lived a long and fruitful life. She was the proud mother of 7 sons and 7 daughters-in-law, as well as numerous grandchildren. That is a lot of family members that could have various opinions on how her estate should have been divided up financially. This did not happen in Elizabeth's family, but sometimes money can drive a wedge between family members who have never had any issues before.

Her mother-in-law had her affairs perfectly organized. She even left hand-written notes to her son who was the Executor of the estate with instructions for closing bank accounts, credit cards, and even magazine subscriptions, immediately upon her death. Everything was in a binder with an up to date will, all investment and bank account information, and her specific desires for family heirlooms. There was absolutely no margin for misunderstanding among any of her heirs. Elizabeth has witnessed what a gift proper estate planning is to the surviving family members and the Executor of the estate, which happened to be her husband. It has inspired her and her husband to make sure their financial affairs are well thought out and organized so their children will not have to worry about anything besides grieving at their deaths as well.

Do you have a current will? If you do have a will, was it originally written and notarized in the state in which you now live? This is one of the biggest mistakes that I encounter when consulting potential clients. They are unaware that if they have moved since they prepared a will, it is no longer applicable in the new state in which they live.

Why is it so important to have a will? It allows you to have sole discretion over the distribution of your assets. You get to decide how your belongings, such as jewelry or family heirlooms, should be distributed when you die. If you have a business or real estate investments, a will also determines who will be the beneficiary of these assets.

The most important reason to have a will if you have minor children, is that it allows you to appoint a guardian whom you know and trust to care for them if you pass away before they are grown adults. If you have children from a prior marriage, even if they are adults, your will can dictate the assets they receive. Having your wishes and desires spelled out specifically in a will also minimizes tensions between survivors. If you are charitably inclined, a will also allows you to gift a pre-determined amount, or percentage of your assets, to the charity of your choice upon your death.

You should also be aware of what a will *cannot* do. Wills normally address the distribution of the majority of your assets, but there are a variety of items that are not covered by the instructions in a will. Such items include:

- Community property
- Proceeds from life insurance policy payouts
- Retirement assets
- Assets owned as joint tenants with rights of survivorship
- Investment accounts that are designated as "transfer on death"

It is very important to make certain that the people you name as beneficiaries of your life insurance policies and your retirement plans, are correct and up to date. I recommend that you review your beneficiary designations for accuracy every two to three years. This is a very expensive mistake that you do not want to make. People often forget whom they originally listed on their life insurance policies, annuities, or retirement accounts as beneficiaries. Then life happens. People divorce and/or remarry. Things change. The worst illustration I have encountered from a financial planning perspective occurred when a gentleman died with a current will, but his life insurance beneficiaries had not been updated in over 20 years. He mistakenly left his life insurance proceeds to an ex-wife rather than his current wife. That is a big *oops*.

If you do NOT have a will when you pass away, you die "intestate," which means that the state government will oversee the distribution of your assets. Contrary to popular opinion, the state does not inherit your assets. However, it will distribute your assets according to a set formula. The formula often results in half of your estate going to your spouse and the other half going to your children. This scenario can result in the sale of the family home, or other assets, which will negatively impact a surviving spouse.

Not having a will can create major financial and emotional difficulties, particularly if your spouse was counting on the bulk of your assets to maintain his or her standard of living. The biggest concern with not having a will arises if your children are minors. The court will appoint a representative to look after your children and their interests. Believe it or not, the number one reason that couples often avoid getting a will is that they cannot agree on a guardian for their children. Rather than coming to a decision, they procrastinate and do not get a will. This is a real travesty if both parents ever die in a common accident, without making proper preparations and plans to take care of their children.

Another common reason people do not get a will is that they are trying to save money. They will tell me, "It is not in the budget right now." I am the biggest proponent you will meet about keeping a close eye on your monthly budget. However, if you die without a will, your lack of preparation will actually cost your heirs a lot of money, time, and heartache, especially if there are disagreements among family members about how your estate should be handled after your death. Wills no longer have to be prepared exclusively by an attorney. You can now get a will by using online software that allows you to customize a legal template to your particular situation. Then you can print the will after it is created on your computer, and simply take it to a bank to have it notarized. You can now get a simple will at www.legaldocs.com or www.legalzoom.com for less than $40.00. There really is no excuse for not getting a will.

Tax considerations are anther very important issue to consider

Proper Estate Planning is a Great Legacy

in order to preserve wealth when preparing your will. Proper estate planning and a well designed will can minimize the tax liability of an individual's estate. Have you ever wondered what the estate tax is and how it may apply to you and your family? The estate tax is a tax on your assets and property before they transfer to your beneficiaries upon your death. The government assesses estate taxes on the total value of your estate. All of the following are included in the value of your estate:

- Your primary residence, net of any mortgage debt
- Investment real estate such as a second home, rental properties, commercial real estate, or land purchased for investment purposes
- Cash, savings accounts, money market accounts, and CDs
- Stocks, bonds, and mutual funds
- Annuities
- Investments in oil and gas or other commodities
- Coin collections
- Jewelry
- Life insurance proceeds
- Business assets
- Other assets of value that an individual may have acquired during their lifetime

The net value of everything you own, regardless of whether the assets have been through probate, is subject to estate taxes. Estate taxes are calculated on the net value of your estate, which includes all your assets less all allowable debts, expenses, and deductions. The most common deductions include the following:

- Mortgage debt
- Administrative expenses for the estate
- The applicable estate tax exemption

After all of the allowable deductions are subtracted from the value of the assets, the resulting taxable value is multiplied by the applicable estate tax rate to determine any taxes owed by the heirs of the estate. The estate tax is also referred to as the death tax. The federal estate tax was first enacted in this country with the Stamp Act of 1797 to help pay for naval rearmament. Over the last century, the laws regarding the estate tax have been through several repeals and reinstatements. The Revenue Act of 1916 finally put the current estate tax into place.[26] Despite its long history, this tax remains very controversial. The argument is that people are being double taxed. They are paying taxes on their income and assets while they are alive, and again when they die.

The most common exception to the federal estate tax is the unlimited marital deduction. The government exempts all transfers of wealth between a husband and wife from federal estate and gift taxes, regardless of the size of the estate. (The surviving spouse must be a U.S. citizen to qualify for this exemption.) However, when the surviving spouse dies, the estate is subject to estate taxes and only the surviving spouse's applicable exemption can be used.

Taxes are an important consideration in distributing your estate because the money your estate pays in taxes will not be available to your heirs. Each estate is allowed a federal estate tax exemption, which is an amount that can pass transfer-tax-free, either through lifetime gifts or at death. The Economic Growth and Tax Relief Reconciliation Act of 2001 gradually increased the federal estate tax exemption until finally repealing the federal estate tax altogether for the 2010 tax year only. The 2010 Tax Relief Act reinstated the federal estate tax with a $5 million exemption (indexed for inflation after 2011) through December 31, 2012. The 2010 estate tax provisions were made permanent by the American Taxpayer Relief Act of 2012, although the top federal estate tax rate was raised to 40%.[27]

The American Taxpayer Relief Act of 2012 extended the federal estate tax with a top tax rate of 40 percent. In 2015, only estates valued at more than $5.43 million (or $10.86 million for some married couples) may be subject to the federal estate tax[28]. If upon your death the total value of your estate is less than the applicable exemption amount, no federal estate taxes will be due. Check with your tax advisor to be sure that your estate is protected as much as possible from estate taxes upon your death.

Year	Exemption Amount	Top Estate Tax Rate
2009	$3.5 million	45%
2010	$0 or $5 million	0% Or 35%
2011	$ 5 million	35%
2012	$ 5.12 million	35%
2013	$5.25 million	40%
2014	$5.34 million	40%
2015	$5.43 million	40%

This material was prepared by Emerald. © 2015 Emerald Connect, LLC[29]

I want to encourage you, my friend, to take time to get your estate planning documents in order. Forbes has created a very thorough list of items that should be addressed in order to leave your heirs the gift of an organized estate. I agree with their recommendations and have included them below for your reference. [30]

Basic Will

A will is the most basic estate-planning document. It outlines who gets your stuff when you die (otherwise the state decides, and it's not always your spouse and/or kids), and who takes care of minor children (otherwise a judge decides). A will also contains the name of your executor, who will administer your estate. Make sure he or she has a copy of your will and other pertinent documents.

Beneficiary Forms

Many people are surprised to find out that the beneficiary forms for life insurance policies and retirement accounts you fill out when you take out the policy or open the account, including

Individual Retirement Accounts and 401(k)s, determine who gets the payouts when you die, unless you've updated it. Not your will. Make sure your beneficiary forms are up to date, and keep copies.

Power of Attorney: Financial
By signing a durable power of attorney, you immediately give another person (your agent) the power to make financial and legal decisions on your behalf. The form can be customized so the agent has more or less power to do things like make annual exclusion gifts or change beneficiary designations on your retirement accounts.

Power of Attorney: Healthcare
A healthcare power of attorney (or health care proxy), authorizes someone (your agent) to make medical decisions for you if you are unable to do so. Please be sure it includes a HIPAA provision, allowing your agent to access your medical information under HIPAA rules.

Living Will
In a living will, also known as an advanced medical directive, you indicate your end of life wishes about prolonging medical care. If you have a chronic illness, consider tailoring it to your specific condition. Also, include an explanation of how to reconcile your choices with any family religious beliefs, if they conflict, to avoid any family discord.

Inventory of Investment Assets
Create a list of all bank accounts, savings accounts, and investment accounts. Be sure to include the account numbers and contact information for the companies servicing your accounts.

List of Contacts
It is a very good idea to type up a list of personal advisors to be included with your will and other estate planning documents.

Include contact information for: lawyers, bankers, financial planners, and tax advisors. In addition, if you own a home, consider making a list of utility and service providers (i.e. lawn care, pest control, magazine subscriptions). Your executor – and your heirs—will thank you.

Guide to Digital Assets

Make a list of your passwords for everything from your credit card accounts to your email accounts. One option is to utilize an online password storage service like: www.my-iwallet.com or keepass.com. Then you only have one password to remember. Give your executor and agent (under your power of attorney) instructions on how to find your password cheat sheet if needed in the future.

Funeral Arrangements

Consider adding a provision in your will stating your desire to be cremated or buried, and where. A separate letter to your heirs in your own handwriting can include details and special wishes. If the letter is handwritten, it is more likely that your wishes will be carried out as you hoped.

Trusts

If you have minor children (under age 18), please be sure your will creates a trust (and names a trustee) for any money left to them. Usually, the trustee is not the same person as the executor of your estate. This provides an extra check and balance.

  Married couples may want to include a bypass or disclaimer trust created on the first spouse's death to preserve his or her estate tax exemption, or to protect the money from going to creditors, and/or a new spouse. The surviving spouse will then have access to the trust's earnings and principal, but what's left in the trust "bypasses" the survivor's estate. Other trusts to consider that a licensed estate-planning attorney can create for you include: irrevocable life insurance trusts, qualified personal residence trusts, grantor-retained annuity trusts, and charitable trusts.

Estate planning is typically the most dreaded aspect of personal financial planning, but it is also one of the most critical aspects of getting your financial affairs in order. Just like having a baby, there will never be a *perfect* time to begin the process of estate planning. If you are single, married with no kids, and/or have a very simple estate, my best advice is to use one of the online resources I mentioned previously to create the required documents. It will be the fastest and least expensive way to go.

However, if you have children, own a business, and/or have significant assets, your best bet is to hire a certified estate-planning attorney that you either know, or has been referred to you by a trusted source. Call today and make an appointment to get the process started if you have not already done so. Then you can check this "to do" off your list and not think about it again. The only exception to this rule is if your circumstances in life change drastically such as marriage, divorce, or the birth of a child. Any time you experience a major change in your life, re-evaluate your will and estate planning documents to make sure they are still relevant and appropriate for your current situation.

15

God Will Provide–It May Just Look Different Than What We Imagined

Search me, O God, and know my heart; test me and know my anxious thoughts.

Psalm 139:23 NIV

My husband and I had the opportunity to travel to Israel as part of our spiritual journey in 2009. We fell in love with Israel and marveled at the opportunity to see the Bible come alive before our very eyes. We truly realized, then, that the stories in the Bible are not fictional. As a Christian, it is impossible to understand the heritage of your own faith if you do not understand the history and culture of the Jewish faith. I am a Judeo-Christian, as are you, if you believe in Jesus Christ as your Lord and Savior.

In order to begin the Holy Week prior to Easter this past year, I attended a Seder dinner, which is the traditional Jewish Passover meal. Toward the end of the Passover meal, the leader who is acting as the priest in a Jewish home will begin to quote and sing the word Dayenu ("die-yay-new"). *Dayenu* means that each act of God would have been enough, and for that alone we should be grateful. For each of His acts of mercy and kindness, we declare "Dayenu."

During the Passover Meal, each of the following statements is read aloud and we all say in Unison, "Dayenu."

Leader: Had God brought us out of Egypt and not divided the

sea for us.
All Respond: "Dayenu."
Leader: Had God divided the sea for us and not sustained us for 40 years in the desert.
All Respond: "Dayenu."
Leader: Had God sustained us for 40 years in the desert and not given us manna.
All Respond: "Dayenu."
Leader: Had God given us the Sabbath and not given us the Torah at Mount Sinai.
All Respond: "Dayenu."
Leader: Had God given us the Torah at Mount Sinai and not led us into the land of Israel.
All Respond: "Dayenu."
Leader: How many and miraculous are the great deeds that our God has performed for us, from taking us out of Egypt to giving us the land of Israel.
All Respond: "Blessed are you, O God, for as you supplied the needs of our ancestors, so do you continue to provide for our needs today."

Beloved, nothing has changed. My friend, Yvette Livesay-Wright, can testify that the God of Israel that provided manna for the Israelites in the desert is the same God today. He is still providing for the needs of each and every one of us. It may look a little differently in our modern culture, but the principles are exactly the same.

Yvette and her husband Michael own a graphic design company. Michael is a very gifted artist and graphic designer. Yvette is very organized, analytical, and an astute businesswoman. They are a great team because their skill sets compliment one another very well. Together, they have learned first hand what it looks like to count their blessings and be completely surrendered to God to provide for their needs.

After many years of praying and waiting for God to reveal his financial plan for them, Michael finally left the security of his full time job to start their own graphic design business in 2011. The first couple of years in particular were very tough financially. Yvette grew more in her faith journey during that year than almost any other time in her life. Yvette is extremely bright, capable, and talented, certainly not a damsel in distress. For her, it was very unsettling to not have financial security. She could not control her destiny just by working harder. Instead she learned dependency on God.

Yvette was kind enough to share her journal with me from the first lean years of their business. She calls it her *Daily Bread Report*. It is her modern day version of "Dayenu," which we now know means that each act of God would have been enough, and for that alone we should be grateful. For each of His acts of mercy and kindness, we declare "Dayenu."

Finances are tough as a new business owner. Michael and Yvette soon learned their clients were not aware of the urgency to pay their bills, even after work had already been completed and invoiced. This attitude was something that they could not control, and it meant they had no steady paycheck coming in on a regular basis. Together, they chose to trust God no matter what. Yvette kept a record of God's faithfulness in their lives through a *Daily Bread Report*. She wrote down the dollar amount, to the penny, that they needed each day to pay a certain bill in black. Then she recorded in red the day that God provided for that particular need, and exactly how much He provided. Honestly, it is completely astounding to see a record of God meeting their needs one step at a time, over and over again. The numbers do not lie.

The following is Yvette's personal testimony:

> *Every time God answered a specific prayer, I wrote it in red so that I couldn't miss it. You can see how much red is on that page. You will also notice that for the most part, God only gave us what we needed, and not much more. Honestly, I appreciate that because it solidified in my mind that God was clearly at work. If you review the report, the amount God blessed us with each time almost matched exactly what the need was. The numbers are so close that I could never mistake God's gifts as a*

coincidence. The report also reminded me on a daily basis that God gives me everything I need daily… just enough for today, like manna for the Israelites. Interestingly, during July and August of 2011, God did not provide according to what I asked for. I knew God was still at work trying to teach me something. The months before when He provided so perfectly for our needs prepared me for this season. A friend wisely brought to my attention the story of Shadrach, Meshach, and Abednego while we were anxiously draining our savings account because no funds were arriving in our mailbox to pay our bills."[31]

Yvette reminded me that in the Book of Daniel, Shadrach, Meshach and Abednego were three young men from Jerusalem condemned to death in a fiery furnace by Nebuchadnezzar, king of Babylon, when they refused to bow down to an image of him and worship any god but the God of Israel. The scriptures in Daniel tell their story of faith:

Shadrach, Meshach and Abednego replied to him, "King Nebuchadnezzar, we do not need to defend ourselves before you in this matter. If we are thrown into the blazing furnace, the God we serve is able to deliver us from it, and he will deliver us from Your Majesty's hand. But even if he does not, we want you to know, Your Majesty, that we will not serve your gods or worship the image of gold you have set up.
Then Nebuchadnezzar was furious with Shadrach, Meshach and Abednego, and his attitude toward them changed. He ordered the furnace heated seven times hotter than usual and commanded some of the strongest soldiers in his army to tie up Shadrach, Meshach and Abednego and throw them into the blazing furnace. So these men, wearing their robes, trousers, turbans and other clothes, were bound and thrown into the blazing furnace. The king's command was so urgent and the

furnace so hot that the flames of the fire killed the soldiers who took up Shadrach, Meshach and Abednego, and these three men, firmly tied, fell into the blazing furnace.

Then King Nebuchadnezzar leaped to his feet in amazement and asked his advisers, "Weren't there three men that we tied up and threw into the fire?" They replied, "Certainly, Your Majesty." He said, "Look! I see four men walking around in the fire, unbound and unharmed, and the fourth looks like a son of the gods."

Nebuchadnezzar then approached the opening of the blazing furnace and shouted, "Shadrach, Meshach and Abednego, servants of the Most High God, come out! Come here!"

So Shadrach, Meshach and Abednego came out of the fire, and the satraps, prefects, governors and royal advisers crowded around them. They saw that the fire had not harmed their bodies, nor was a hair of their heads singed; their robes were not scorched, and there was no smell of fire on them. Then Nebuchadnezzar said, "Praise be to the God of Shadrach, Meshach and Abednego, who has sent his angel and rescued his servants! They trusted in him and defied the king's command and were willing to give up their lives rather than serve or worship any god except their own God. (Daniel 3:16-28 NIV)

Yvette continued to tell me how much the story of Shadrach, Meshach and Abednego really resonated with her. She says that she has never forgotten it. "When we first started our business, I knew that God was able to bring the money in, but even if He didn't, He was still my God and I would still worship Him."

Take a moment to remember the ways that God has provided for your needs and, most likely, many of your wants throughout your life. It is very encouraging to look back and see all of the many ways that God has blessed us and watched over us, even when the circumstances were the toughest. You may want to start a *Daily Bread Report* just like my friend Yvette. Then you will also have a written testimony of God's faithfulness in your life. Remember, you can take heart that our God is fully sovereign and in control of the universe. You can trust Him!

> **Prov 30:8b** – Give me neither poverty nor riches, but give me only my daily bread.
>
> In these times remember Shadrach, Meshach & Abednego
>
> **Daniel 3:17,18**
> If we are thrown into the blazing furnace, the God we serve IS ABLE to deliver us from your Majesty's hand. But even if he does not, we want you to know, Your Majesty, that we will not serve your gods or worship the image of gold you have set up.

DAILY BREAD REPORT

Need	Date Received	Amount Received
$4,000 by 2/28/11	2/27/11	$4,193.46
$2,500 by 3/5/11	3/4/11	$1,582.46
$1,070 today 3/7/11	3/7/11	$1,101.82
$1,360 by 3/10/11	3/10/11	$1,372.74
$1,670 by 3/21/11	3/21/11	$5,198.23
$1,200 by 3/29/11	3/31/11	$1,332.18
$600 by 4/18/11	4/14/11	$766.18
$2,400 by 4/20/11	4/19/11	$2,779.10
$2,200 by 4/21/11	4/22/11	$2,698.87
$3,300 by 5/2/11	5/2/11	$2,850.00
$3,740 by 5/30/11	5/29/11	$857.34
$750 by 6/16/11	6/16/11	$450.00
$6,500 by 6/30/11	6/30/11	$6,513.74
$4,000 by 7/5/11	7/5/11	$1,126.88
$260 by 7/7/11		$0.00
$1,100 by 8/5/11		drained all savings except one account
$700 by 8/8/11	8/8/11	$727.00
$865 week of 8/11/11	8/11/11	$2,852.54
$6,400 by 9/30/11	9/21/11	$6,580.81
$3,000 by 10/31/11	11/1/11	$3,476.72

CONCLUSION

I pray that the eyes of your heart may be enlightened in order that you may know the hope to which He has called you, the riches of his glorious inheritance in his holy people.

Ephesians 1:18 NIV

This is my prayer for you: *that the eyes of your heart may be enlightened.* I hope you will pray about the financial topics discussed in this book. Then determine which positive steps forward you need to take today. Friend, the choice is yours. Will you live in fear as it is relates to your finances? *Or* will you choose to be proactive with personal financial planning for you and your loved ones?

I encourage you to seek wise counsel and develop a financial plan for your future so you have direction. Every one of us needs a road map in life so we know where we are headed. Life will happen, and you will have to adjust your financial plan accordingly. Remember to be flexible.

Your first goal should be to make sure you have a cash reserve. Then assess your savings goals and needs, such as retirement and/or college planning, if you have not already done so. Start a realistic savings plan to meet your goals and commit to honor it every month. Take inventory of your spending habits. Do you have credit card debt that needs to be eliminated so you will not feel enslaved to the lender? Maybe you're still trying to fill your heart with objects of this world and not God's love for you.

One of the practical aspects of financial planning we discussed in this book is the need for insurance. Do you have life insurance and a current will in order to make sure that your children and spouse are taken care of in the event of your death? Is your ability to generate an income insured with a disability income insurance policy? Remember, while you are still healthy and able to go to work, your biggest financial asset is your ability to work and create wealth. Have you determined whether or not you or your parents need Long Term Care Insurance to cover the cost of any unforeseen medical care in the future?

Have you started to give to your church and to others that are in need? We live in the richest country in the world. However, there is still suffering and unmet needs all around us. Please, please know that work is honorable and noble. It allows us to provide for our families. However, your family's needs are not the only needs in the world. Providing for your family is your first priority and then beyond that, there's a whole world of need out there.

Friend, do not feel guilty about making money. If you allow guilt to motivate you, then you will sabotage your own success by letting your subconscious tell you that you are doing something wrong because you're making money. The Bible says that money *can* be a root of evil. It does not say that it *is* the root of all evil. Money can be misused, but it's not the problem. The problem is actually a heart issue. This is an issue to be worked out between you and God. Be honest with yourself. Answer the following questions:

What am I doing with my money?

Am I being a wise steward, or investor, of the assets that God has given me?

In our world today, there is a false association between wealth and greed. Some of the poorest people in the world may be the greediest people you will meet. Some of the wealthiest people in the world may be the most generous. These facts may sound politically incorrect or controversial. However, greedy people covet what other people have, but they are not willing to work for money. Wealth comes with responsibility. It has the potential to change the trajectory of the future for yourself, your family, as well as other people and missions that you give to in this world.

What are you really passionate about? Educating people? Providing clean water for those who don't have access to clean water for their families? Spreading the gospel of Jesus Christ? The money you give away generously and strategically to nonprofit ministries in this world can have a ripple effect on bettering our world and the kingdom of God. The more money you make, the more impact you can have.

Accumulating money is not something to feel guilty about; it's an honorable thing. Giving of your time by volunteering is noble. However, your time is a finite resource. You *cannot* volunteer indefinitely. You can have far more of an impact in this world if you use your time and gifts to generate money in order to support those already working in the mission field. They are far better equipped to run their non-profit organizations than you are. Remember we discussed the roles of kings and priests in Chapter 4. Prayerfully ask God to reveal to you what your specific role is in His kingdom. Trust me, we are all an important part of the Body of Christ.

Friend, the same God that brought the Israelites out of Egypt is the same God that we worship today. He wants to bless you. He wants a relationship with you. He will provide for your needs. But most of all, He wants your heart.

I'm so excited to see where this new journey to financial freedom takes you. May you be blessed richly both in this life and eternally as well. If you have accepted Jesus Christ as your personal Lord and Savior, then your life really is insured. I pray that you spend eternity with our very good God. As they say in the military right before they embark on an important mission, see you on the flipside!

ACKNOWLEDGMENTS

Thanks to my father, you taught me how to love God, serve others, and be an entrepreneur. Thank you for teaching me that I can persevere and overcome many challenges, as long as God is the anchor of my life. You have always been my biggest cheerleader.

Thanks to my mother, you taught me the power of prayer and how to be a Godly wife and mother. You are the picture of grace during challenging health situations. I love you fiercely.

Thanks to my brother, you are a steady, Godly warrior for your family and your church. I admire your leadership, wisdom, and integrity. As my much older brother, there is no doubt that you have kept me humble!

Thanks to my husband, you are my best friend, my encourager, and the love of my life. You have walked through valleys and climbed mountains with me. I thank God that you are my partner in this life.

Thanks to my daughter, you have forever changed me. You are beautiful inside and out. You are a natural born leader. Always let your light shine for Jesus. Follow your passions. Be the change this world needs.

Thanks to my son, we prayed for you for years. You completed our family. I love your smile, your sense of humor, and your gentle spirit. You are a blessing to all who meet you. Be strong and courageous! Always seek God and He will make your path straight.

ENDNOTES

[1] Serenity prayer. It was originally written by Reinhold Niebuhr

[2] Franklin, Benjamin.

[3] Source of Budget Worksheet: Pivotal Financial Advisors, LLC.

[4] Statistics from TransUnion and Experian analysis of May 2013 credit files. (http://www.creditcards.com/credit-card-news/credit-card-industry-facts-personal-debt-statistics-1276)

[5] Mother Teresa. (http://www.quotationspage.com/quote/30075.html)

[6] Ziglar, Zig. Newsletter, Edition #35, on August 31, 2010. (http://www.ziglar.com/newsletter/august-31-2010-edition-35)

[7] Warren, Rick. October 24, 2013. He is the founder of Pastors.com, a global Internet community for pastors. (http://pastors.com/8-reasons-believers-give-to-your-church)

[8] High, David R., *Kings and Priests*. (Publisher: Books for Children of the World, Oklahoma City, OK, 1993, page 7)

[9] Tara Parker-Pope/ Wall Street Journal, December 6, 2005 (http://www.mindfully.org/Health/2005/Shopping-Dopamine-Junkie6dec05.htm)

[10] "Balloon Payment "Definition. Wikipedia. October 2010. (https://en.wikipedia.org/wiki/Balloon_payment_mortgage)

[11] Definition of "Steward". Webster's 1913 Dictionary. (http://www.webster-dictionary.org/definition/steward)

[12] Benjamin Franklin, *The Pall Mall Magazine* (September 1899), 107

[13] *Definition of "Mutual Fund"*. Investopedia. (http://www.investopedia.com/articles/mutualfund/05/071305.asp)

[14] Kennon, Joshua. Bonds 101:What They Are and How They Work. (http://beginnersinvest.about.com/cs/bondbasics/f/whatisabond.htm)

[15] Siebold, Steve, "How Rich People Think", June 25, 2014 (http://www.businessinsider.com/rich-people-teach-their-kids-to-be-rich-2015-9)

[16] *"Asset Allocation Definition" Investopedia*. 19 Nov 2003, (http://www.investopedia.com/terms/a/assetallocation.asp)

[17] Article written by Mylestone Plans, Financial Services Firm located in Rockville, MD. (http://www.mylestoneplans.com/New-Flexibility-for-College-Savings.c6628.htm)

[18] Hyland, Timothy. President of Stone Hill Financial, LLC in Annandale, NJ. Newsletter located on the following website: http://www.stonehillfinancial.net/New-Flexibility-for-College-Savings.c6628.htm

[19] Maimonides. He was a famous Spanish Philosopher born on March 30, 1135. (http://www.brainyquote.com)

[20] Hatmaker, Jen, *Guideposts*: Interview on July 15, 2015.

[21] Lucado, Max, *Come Thirsty*: (Thomas Nelson, Nashville, Tennessee, 2011, page 108).

[22] Trent Fielder. Email date: September 9, 2015.

[23] United States Census Bureau, July 25, 2012. (www.census.gov/newsroom)

[24] This quiz was written and prepared by Emerald. Copyright 2015 Emerald Connect, LLC.

[25] Source: LIMRA, 2014.

[26] Katrenia R. Collins, L.L.C., Attorney at Law in Atlanta, GA. (http://www.krclawoffice.com/Estate-Tax.c1284.htm)

[27] Carr, Richard. He is President of Carr Financial Group located in Worcester, MA. (http://www.carrfinancial.net/Estate-Tax.c1284.htm)

[28] This material was written and prepared by Emerald Connect, LLC. © 2015 Emerald Connect, LLC.

[29] This material was prepared by Emerald. © 2015 Emerald Connect, LLC. It is not intended to replace investment or tax advice for your financial situation.

[30] Forbes.com, "10 Must Have Estate Planning Documents." (http://www.forbes.com/pictures/mjh45imjf/basic-will)

[xxxii] Yvette's Livesay-Wright, September 9, 2015.

Emily Graham Stroud lives in Fort Worth, Texas with her husband and two children. Just like many women today, she wears a lot of hats. She owns and manages a boutique investment firm called Stroud Financial Management. In her personal life, Emily is a wife, mother, daughter, sister, friend, and she is passionate about Jesus. In her work life, she counsels people on how to handle their wealth, manage risk, and ensure a nice tidy retirement. Emily does her best to beat the odds of the stock market. She helps her clients plan and mitigate each possible financial scenario that can arise in their life.

Most importantly, Emily sincerely desires to take care of her clients and her family. She wants them all to thrive financially, emotionally, and spiritually. She is dedicated to providing both her clients and her readers with clear, easily understood explanations of financial products and services.

Emily Graham Stroud, MBA, CFA
President and Owner of Stroud Financial Management, Inc.

EDUCATION:
Bachelor's, Texas A&M University;
Masters of Business Administration, Finance Concentration, Texas Christian University.

AWARDS/HONORS:
Chartered Financial Analyst (CFA), 2002.

PROFESSIONAL MEMBERSHIPS/AFFILIATIONS:
Member of the Association for Investment Management and Research;
Financial Planning Association memberships;
She is fully licensed with FINRA and the Texas State Securities Board to sell securities;
Texas State Board of Insurance licensed; and a
Cambridge Investment Research, Inc. Registered Representative.*

*Emily G. Stroud is a Registered Representative. Securities offered through Cambridge Investment Research, Inc., a Broker/Dealer, Member FINRA/SIPC. Investment Advisor Representative Cambridge Investment Research Advisors, Inc., a Registered Investment Advisor. Cambridge and Emily G. Stroud, LLC are not affiliated.